ROBIN WILLIAMS

OVERCOMING ADVERSITY

ROBIN WILLIAMS

Hal Marcovitz

Introduction by James Scott Brady,
Trustee, the Center to Prevent Handgun Violence
Vice Chairman, the Brain Injury Foundation

Chelsea House Publishers
Philadelphia

Frontis: *Robin Williams gives one of the over-the-top perfor-mances that have characterized his work both as a comedian and an actor since he emerged as a star in the late 1970s.*

CHELSEA HOUSE PUBLISHERS

EDITOR IN CHIEF Stephen Reginald
PRODUCTION MANAGER Pamela Loos
ART DIRECTOR Sara Davis
DIRECTOR OF PHOTOGRAPHY Judy L. Hasday
MANAGING EDITOR James D. Gallagher
SENIOR PRODUCTION EDITOR J. Christopher Higgins

Staff for **ROBIN WILLIAMS**
ASSOCIATE ART DIRECTOR Takeshi Takahashi
DESIGNER Takeshi Takahashi
PICTURE RESEARCHER Lynn Isaacson Fairbanks
COVER ILLUSTRATOR Robert Gerson

The Chelsea House World Wide Web site address is:
http://www.chelseahouse.com

First Printing

1 3 5 7 9 8 6 4 2

Library of Congress Cataloging-in-Publication Data applied for
ISBN 0-7910-5308-3 (hc)
       0-7910-5309-1 (pb)

LCCN 00-025813

CONTENTS

OVERCOMING ADVERSITY

TIM ALLEN
comedian/performer

MAYA ANGELOU
author

APOLLO 13 MISSION
astronauts

LANCE ARMSTRONG
professional cyclist

DREW BARRYMORE
actress

JAMES BRADY
gun control activist

DREW CAREY
comedian/performer

JIM CARREY
comedian/performer

BILL CLINTON
U.S. president

TOM CRUISE
actor

MICHAEL J. FOX
actor

WHOOPI GOLDBERG
comedian/performer

EKATERINA GORDEEVA
figure skater

SCOTT HAMILTON
figure skater

JEWEL
singer and poet

JAMES EARL JONES
actor

QUINCY JONES
musician and producer

ABRAHAM LINCOLN
U.S. president

WILLIAM PENN
Pennsylvania's founder

JACKIE ROBINSON
baseball legend

ROSEANNE
entertainer

MONICA SELES
tennis star

SAMMY SOSA
baseball star

DAVE THOMAS
entrepreneur

SHANIA TWAIN
entertainer

ROBIN WILLIAMS
performer

STEVIE WONDER
entertainer

ON FACING ADVERSITY

James Scott Brady

I GUESS IT'S a long way from a Centralia, Illinois, train yard to the George Washington University Hospital Trauma Unit. My dad was a yardmaster for the old Chicago, Burlington & Quincy Railroad. As a child, I used to get to sit in the engineer's lap and imagine what it was like to drive that train. I guess I always have liked being in the "driver's seat."

Years later, however, my interest turned from driving trains to driving campaigns. In 1979, former Texas governor John Connally hired me as a press secretary in his campaign for the American presidency. We lost the Republican primary to a former Hollywood star named Ronald Reagan. But I managed to jump over to the Reagan campaign. When Reagan was elected in 1980, I was "sitting in the catbird seat," as humorist James Thurber would say—poised to be named presidential press secretary. I held that title throughout the eight years of the Reagan administration. But not without one terrible, extended interruption.

It happened barely two months after the Reagan administration took office. I never even heard the shots. On March 30, 1981, my life went blank in an instant. In an attempt to assassinate President Reagan, John Hinckley Jr. armed himself with a "Saturday night special"—a low-quality, $29 pistol and shot wildly as our presidential entourage exited a Washington hotel. One of the exploding bullets struck me just above the left eye. It shattered into a couple dozen fragments, some of which penetrated my skull and entered my brain.

7

The next few months of my life were a nightmare of repeated surgery, broken contact with the outside world, and a variety of medical complications. More than once, I was very close to death.

The next few years were filled with frustrating struggles to function with a paralyzed right side, struggles to speak and communicate.

To people who face and defeat daunting obstacles, "ambition" is not becoming wealthy or famous or winning elections or awards. Words like "ambition" and "achievement" and "success" take on very different meanings. The objective is just to live, to wake up every morning. The goals are not lofty; they are very ordinary.

My own heroes are ordinary folks—but they accomplish extraordinary things because they try. My greatest hero is my wife, Sarah. She's accomplished a lot of things in life, but two stand out. The first has been the way she has cared for me and our son since I was shot. A tremendous tragedy and burden was dropped unexpectedly into her life, totally beyond her control and without justification. She could have given up; instead, she focused her energies on preserving our family and returning our lives to normal as much as possible. Week by week, month by month, year by year, she has not reached for the miraculous, just for the normal. Yet in focusing on the normal, she has helped accomplish the miraculous.

Her other most remarkable accomplishment, to me, has been spearheading the effort to keep guns out of the hands of criminals and children in America. Opponents call her a "gun grabber"; I call her a national hero. And I am not alone.

After a seven-year battle, during which Sarah and I worked tirelessly to educate the public about the need for stronger gun laws, the Brady Bill became law in 1993. It was a victory, achieved in the face of tremendous opposition, that now benefits all Americans. From the time the law took effect through fall 1997, background checks had stopped 173,000 criminals and other high-risk purchasers from buying handguns, and the law has helped to reduce illegal gun trafficking.

Sarah was not pursuing fame, or even recognition. She simply started at one point—when our son, Scott, found a loaded handgun on the seat of a pickup truck and, thinking it was a toy, pointed it at Sarah.

Fortunately, no one was hurt. But seeing a gun nearly bring a second tragedy upon our family, Sarah became determined to do whatever she could to prevent senseless death and injury from guns.

Some people think of Sarah as a powerful political force. To me, she's the person who so many times fed me and helped me dress during my long years of recovery.

Overcoming obstacles is part of life, not just for people who are challenged by disabilities, illnesses, or tragedies, but for all people. No matter what the obstacle—fear, disability, prejudice, grief, or a difficulty that isn't likely to "just go away"—we can all work to make this world a better place.

An excited Robin Williams serenades his Oscar statuette. He won the award in 1998 as Best Supporting Actor for his part in the film Good Will Hunting.

1
THE FUNNIEST MAN IN AMERICA

AS HOLLYWOOD'S DAZZLING STARS and starlets filed into the prestigious Shrine Auditorium in Los Angeles on Oscar night in 1998, there was little doubt in their minds about what was going to happen in the next few hours.

Titanic, the blockbuster film of the year, was almost sure to garner a record number of Academy Awards. The disaster epic, which had cost $200 million to make and had earned more than double that amount, was nominated in most of the major categories; after all, a major studio campaign had been under way for weeks to make certain the film would sweep the Oscars.

But although *Titanic* was the heavy favorite to take home a great number of Academy Award statuettes, the makers of another film were also hoping for recognition by the Academy. *Good Will Hunting* was the story of a rebellious and underachieving mathematical genius and the psychotherapist who coaxed him out of his shell. This therapist was played by Robin Williams, the veteran actor and comedy star who had come very close to winning Oscars in his career three times before.

Each time before, though, Robin had just missed.

Millions of television sets were tuned to the Academy Awards that night in 1998. Within the Shrine Auditorium, a silence fell over the crowd as presenter Mira Sorvino spoke:

"The nominees are. . .

"Greg Kinnear for *As Good As It Gets.*

"Burt Reynolds for *Boogie Nights.*

"Anthony Hopkins for *Amistad.*

"Robert Forster for *Jackie Brown.*

"And Robin Williams for *Good Will Hunting.*"

The race for Best Supporting Actor was one of the dramas that had dominated Oscar talk all spring. Since no actor from *Titanic* had been nominated in that category, Oscar handicappers had declared the race wide open.

Still, Burt Reynolds seemed to have an edge on the other actors. Reynolds, who played adult film director Jack Horner in *Boogie Nights,* was a veteran actor with a long list of movie and TV credits. Reynolds had seen his popularity wane in recent years due to a series of box-office flops, but *Boogie Nights* was regarded as his comeback role. Reynolds was definitely the sentimental favorite, and in the weeks leading up to Oscar night he took a step ahead of the competition when he captured the Golden Globe Award for his role. (Golden Globes are awarded by the Hollywood Press Association, an organization of critics who work for magazines, newspapers, and other media outlets.)

Few people, however, would have argued with the outcome if one of the other nominees in the Supporting Actor field captured the Oscar. Hopkins had already won the 1992 Best Actor award for his chilling portrayal of Hannibal Lecter in the psychological thriller *Silence of the Lambs.* (Ironically, he had beaten Robin out of the Oscar that year, when Robin was also nominated as Best Actor for his role in *The Fisher King.*) Greg Kinnear was an enormously popular TV star who had made the transition to feature film work by scoring an Oscar nomination in one of his first roles. And Robert Forster was regarded as one of the true anchors of *Jackie Brown,* the violent crime drama directed by Quentin Tarantino.

Faced with that competition, Robin regarded himself as a long shot. "The Oscar nominations are a great stroke," he told an interviewer for *Hollywood Online* shortly before the awards ceremony. "I'm not going to lie. It's a great honor, to go into a room and see Jack Nicholson and Dustin Hoffman sitting there, all these amazing actors. It would be great to win, but I'm not betting on myself."

The nominees sat patiently through the program while they listened to the host for the telecast, Billy Crystal, an actor and comedian who was Robin's close friend. They heard Stanley Donen, who directed and choreographed many of the blockbuster Hollywood musicals of the 1940s and 1950s, receive an honorary Oscar for his lifetime of work. They listened as Fay Wray, who starred in the 1933 classic *King Kong,* was also singled out for recognition.

Titanic did not disappoint its fans. The film won 11 Oscar trophies that night, tying the record held by the 1959 epic *Ben Hur.* James Cameron, the director of *Titanic,* accepted the Oscar for best director by shouting the most popular line from his movie: "I'm the king of the world!"

Then, as the evening wore on, *Good Will Hunting* captured the Oscar for Best Original Screenplay. The movie's writers were Matt Damon and Ben Affleck, the two young actors who also starred in the film. Without a doubt, *Good Will Hunting* owed much of its success to their creative genius, but the movie also owed no small debt to Robin Williams.

Damon and Affleck wrote the character of Sean Maguire, the therapist, with Williams in mind, but they had no guarantee that Robin would be drafted for the role. In fact the film was in trouble until Robin stepped in and agreed to play Maguire. Affleck and Damon had first found a buyer for their script in Castle Rock Pictures. The

Robin as teacher and thera-
pist Sean Maguire in a scene
from Good Will Hunting.
While Williams made his mark
as a comedian, there was
nothing funny about the way
he played this dramatic role.

studio balked, though, at giving the two young actors top roles in the film. (Damon intended to play Will Hunting, the mathematical genius, while Affleck expected to be cast as Will's friend Chuckie.) Instead, Castle Rock insisted that two better-known actors be found for the starring roles. Affleck and Damon next took their script to Miramax Films, which agreed to let Damon and Affleck remain in the key roles—as long as Robin Williams played Maguire. Luckily for Affleck and Damon, Robin accepted.

"I was amazed to meet Matt and Ben, both of whom are in their early 20s, and discover they had written this really complex piece," Robin told reporters shortly after the film was released. "The movie is about a damaged genius who is changed by his encounters with my character—a therapist who is damaged in another way.

"It's a tough piece. The therapist is a guy who grew up in South Boston and he's got an edge to him. The guy takes the punches and comes back because he's determined to make a connection. I had a blast making this movie."

The gamble certainly paid off for Miramax. Made on a small budget, *Good Will Hunting* earned an astonishing $133 million at the box office.

When at last it was time to give out the Oscar for Best Supporting Actor, Robin certainly knew the routine; he had already been through the tension of Oscar night three times before. Each of those evenings, he had to remain in the audience while other actors went to the podium to accept their honors. His face would appear in a split-screen on TV as the camera captured the reactions of the winner as well as the other four nominated actors who would have to take their disappointment with good sportsmanship.

But on this early spring night in 1998, Robin Williams finally found himself at the pinnacle of his career.

The envelope was opened.

"And the winner is. . .

"Robin Williams!"

Robin embraced his wife Marsha and then shot out of his seat and hurried to the stage. He hugged Billy Crystal. Flustered, he graciously accepted his statuette, but he couldn't resist the temptation to make a little joke.

"Thank you. Oh, man. This might be the one time I'm speechless," he said. "Oh, thank you so much for this incredible honor. Thank you for putting me in a category with these four extraordinary men."

Robin shot a glance into the auditorium, where the cast of *Good Will Hunting* was seated. "Ben and Matt, I still

Matt Damon (left) and Ben Affleck, who won Oscars for the screenplay of Good Will Hunting, *had written the part of Sean Maguire with Robin Williams in mind. Damon and Affleck also starred in the film, which was one of the biggest hits of 1998, earning more than $130 million at the box office.*

want to see some I.D.," he said, poking fun at the ages of the film's two big stars.

Robin then took a moment to speak about his father, who had died in 1987. Although Robin and his father had a distant relationship early on, as Robin grew older, father and son became closer. In fact, Robert Williams had supported his son financially for months while Robin was trying to establish himself on the stand-up comedy circuit.

Of course he thanked his father in the only way he knew how—with a touch of comedy.

"And most of all," Robin told the audience in the Shrine Auditorium, "I want to thank my father up there, the man who when I said I wanted to be an actor, he said, 'Wonderful, just have a backup profession like welding.' Thank you. God bless you."

A clean-cut Robin Williams, in a photo taken while he was a junior at the Detroit Country Day School in Michigan. Just six years later, Robin would find himself learning acting in New York, and working outside the Metropolitan Museum of Art as a street mime.

2

THE STREET MIME

THE METROPOLITAN MUSEUM of Art is an imposing edifice in midtown Manhattan, its Greco-Roman columns towering high above Fifth Avenue. Inside, visitors will find some of the world's most renowned art treasures: paintings by such modern European masters as Pablo Picasso and Henri Matisse, as well as works by classical artists such as Rembrandt and Rodin. A visitor would need to traipse up and down the Metropolitan's polished marble corridors for days before he or she could see all the thousands of items in the museum's magnificent collection.

But the Metropolitan is more than just a museum. It is the centerpiece of New York's cultural world, located along one of the Big Apple's busiest and classiest streets. Each day thousands of people congregate out front on the Metropolitan's concrete steps or on the sprawling urban mall that runs the length of the huge building.

Of course, wherever you find that many people in a big city you'll find street vendors. They are a big part of the hustle and bustle of any big city, familiar and friendly additions to the urban pulse. Some street vendors in New York sell souvenirs of the city, small cast-iron replicas of the Statue of Liberty or the Empire State Building (molded, of course, in Hong Kong). Some of the vendors sell T-shirts and headbands or scarves and sunglasses. Others sell hot dogs and sodas or the ethnic foods favored by New York's diverse international population.

Some of the street vendors, however, aren't really vendors at all. Rather, they work as street mimes, painting their faces white—in the tradition of the harlequins of the medieval European stage—and then acting out little comedies in pantomime (a style of acting that requires the mime to tell the story without speaking or using props). A visitor might see a street mime act out the story of a man trapped in a box; the mime feels with his hands the broad, slippery sides of the box, but despite jumping in place or making hand-over-hand motions with his arms, he is unable to climb out of the box. Or a mime might act intoxicated on liquor and drag his body sluggishly across the Metropolitan's hard steps. Even the simple act of drinking a glass of water can bring a chuckle from the crowd. (Of course, the mime has to quench his thirst without the benefit of a real glass or, indeed, real water.)

Back in 1974, one of the street mimes who regularly plied his trade on the steps of the Metropolitan Museum of Art was Robin Williams. The job didn't pay much, to be sure, a dollar here and there from a tourist, or perhaps spare change from a Metropolitan Museum tour guide who would sit on the steps on a spring lunch hour, enjoying the sunshine while the funny little man in white pancake makeup made him laugh. Still, it was money. Despite the fact that Robin Williams was born to wealth, he had decided to make a go of it in New York on his own, without the financial help of his parents, Robert and Laurie Williams.

Miming on the steps of the Metropolitan in 1974, Robin Williams had come a long way from his home in California.

*   *   *

When Robin was born on July 21, 1952, his family lived near Chicago, Illinois, but they would soon move to Bloomfield Hills, Michigan, a suburb of Detroit populated mostly by automotive company executives and their families.

Robin's father, Robert Williams, was a vice president of the Ford Motor Company, which in the early 1950s had decided to challenge General Motors for a larger share of the American luxury car market. GM's entry in the field was the pricey Cadillac, the car for the rich man. Ford countered with the Lincoln Continental, and Robert Williams's job was to supervise sales of Lincolns throughout the Midwest.

Robert Williams had been born to money in his own right, but Robin's father still knew tough times. When he was a teenager, his family business went bankrupt and the young man was forced to work in a coal mine. Later, Robert served in the Navy in World War II and narrowly escaped death when a Japanese airplane crashed into his ship. Perhaps these experiences hardened him. At any rate, he came across as a cold, rigid man.

By the early 1950s, Robert Williams had met and married his second wife, Laurie. She had two children from a previous marriage. By this time, Robert had become very successful at Ford. He was 46 years old when his son Robin was born.

With his father on the road a great deal and his mother involved in society functions, as well as her occasional work as a model, young Robin was lonely in the large mansion where he grew up. To compensate for his loneliness, Robin developed his imagination. He made up imaginary friends and gave them all their own unique voices. He also spent a lot of time playing hide-and-seek with the family dog, Duke. Another of Robin's favorite pastimes was to hide out in the attic, playing with his enormous

Laurie Williams attends an entertainment function with her famous son. Robin had a warm relationship with his mother, but his father, Robert Williams, often seemed cold and distant when Robin was growing up.

army of toy soldiers. He had time-machine battles, with Confederate soldiers fighting GIs carrying automatic weapons, or medieval knights fighting Nazis. Robin was already exhibiting the creativity that he would later put to use in his career.

Robin did have two half brothers, Todd and Lauren, but they were both much older than he. "There were no other kids in the neighborhood," Robin told an interviewer for *Playboy* magazine in 1982. "There was nobody around to play with. . . . My half brothers, Todd and Lauren, were a lot older than I and I didn't see them until I was around ten. Todd always extorted all my money. He'd come into my room and say he needed some beer money, and I'd say, 'Oh, gosh, yes, take it all.' My mother would get furious, because Todd would get into my piggy bank and walk out with $40 worth of pennies." Obviously, Robin and his half brothers were not close.

As a young child, Robin was not close to his parents either. "My father was away, my mother was working, doing benefits," he told *Esquire* magazine in 1989. "I was basically raised by this maid, and my mother would come in later, you know, and I knew her, and she was wonderful and charming and witty."

Robin's father was stern, demanding, and humorless. He expected perfect performance at school, but no matter how hard Robin worked, no matter how many A's he received on his report card, he was never certain he had done enough to please his father. As a boy, Robin yearned for his father's praise. Robert Williams's life, however, had been built on hard work, discipline, and self-control. He had little time for his young son. And he had even less time for his son's developing sense of humor.

Robin soon learned that his mother, however, loved to laugh—and the way for him to be close to her was to make her laugh. In fact, he became quite good at it. "I think maybe comedy was part of my way of connecting with my mother," he told *Esquire*. "I'll make Mommy laugh and that'll be okay."

As he continually thought up new ways to amuse his mother, Robin discovered the gift of mimicry. He was very good at imitating not only the sounds but also the physical nuances of different people. One of Robin's favorite targets for mimicry was his father. If he became too loud and rambunctious, however, his mother would quickly shush him. Still longing to please both his father and his mother, Robin would go to his room to study diligently for his next test at school.

Years later, however, after Robin made his mark as an international movie star, he would insist in interview after interview that he knew nothing but love and devotion from his father—even though Robert Williams was hardly a warm and loving man. In fact, as a boy, Robin had a nickname for his father: he called him Lord Stokesbury, Viceroy to India. But never to his face, of course; the young boy was too intimidated.

When he wasn't studying or playing games of make believe, Robin read books and watched television, that new form of entertainment that had found its way into American homes during the 1950s. Robin became a fan of *The Jack Paar Show,* a late-night television variety show in the early 1960s. Robin was particularly mesmerized whenever the Paar show would feature a rotund and zany comedian named Jonathan Winters. The comic mastery of Winters left a deep and lasting impression on young Robin.

Meanwhile Robin was having trouble fitting in at school. By his own admission, he was short, fat, and shy. He found himself bullied by bigger kids.

"Mom and Dad had put me in a public school, and most of the kids there were bigger than me and wanted to prove they were bigger by throwing me into walls," Robin told *Playboy* in 1982. "There were a lot of burly farm kids and sons of auto plant workers there, and I'd come to school looking for new entrances and thinking, 'If only I could come in through the roof.' They'd nail me as soon as I'd go through the door."

As he grew older, Robin developed two strategies to take care of his antagonists. First he decided to develop himself as an athlete. He took up wrestling and cross-country running. The wrestling toned his body and developed his muscles, making him much harder to push around. The long-distance running helped slim his waist and developed his self-confidence. Robin's second strategy developed when he found out that if he made other

people laugh, they wouldn't be quite so hostile to him. Soon the beatings from the older boys stopped.

Robin moved on to Detroit Country Day School in nearby Birmingham, Michigan, a private school where he was forced to wear a blazer and school tie every day. He found the atmosphere restrictive, but he made the best of it. He also joined the wrestling team and found success, eventually moving to the state finals where he ultimately lost to a much more experienced wrestler.

By 1969 Robert Williams had had enough of the auto industry. He was upset by its declining values and the drive by senior management to make money by cutting corners and shortchanging the consumer on quality. So he took an early retirement from Ford and moved his family to the small northern California town of Tiburon in Marin

In school, Robin became involved in several sports, and became very successful as a wrestler, reaching the state finals in his junior year. Here, Robin (top) works to turn an opponent.

A photo of Robin from his senior year at Redwood High School. His family had moved from Michigan to California after his junior year. Robin found life much different in his new home, Tiburon, a suburb of San Francisco.

County. Robin suddenly found himself free of the buttoned-down world of Bloomfield Hills. Northern California in 1969 was home to the laid-back counterculture of long-haired flower children in blue jeans, love beads, and Hawaiian shirts.

And drugs.

Not cocaine, of course. This was still 1969 and cocaine was not yet the illegal drug of choice for young people out for a high. Besides, it was too expensive for most high school kids. No, when Robin Williams was in high school young people smoked marijuana and "dropped acid," meaning they swallowed capsules of lysergic acid diethylamide—otherwise known as LSD.

Robin found himself fitting right in.

"It was wonderful—and very, very weird," Robin recalled in 1982. "I went to Redwood High School, which had courses in 16mm film making and a lot of psychology-type classes. It was the height of the encounter period, and in a lot of classes, teachers would get everybody together for an energy hug. I remember one teacher would sometimes just stop what he was doing and then a few kids would start pounding out a beat and everybody would get up and dance around the room. There was also a black-studies department, even though there was only one black kid in the school—and he didn't want any part of it. He said, 'I know I'm black, so just leave me alone and let me go to school. I don't have to be in no black-studies program.'

"It was incredible to go from a private all-boys' high school to a place where there were Gestalt history classes and where kids were always flying around on acid. The first time I walked into one of the bathrooms, a bunch of guys were in there, all spaced out. One kid took me aside and whispered, 'Don't wake them.' I didn't."

Robin soon found himself dropping his private school habits. "At first, I still carried my briefcase," he told *Playboy,* "and guys would either ask, 'Who's the geek?' or stare at me and say, 'Wow, a briefcase—how unmellow. You're really creating negative energy.' In the Midwest, if your classmates thought you were creating negative energy, you'd hear, 'Yo!' followed by a right cross to the jaw. It took me a few weeks before I showed up at Redwood High without a tie on, and within a couple of months, I finally took the big step and went to school in jeans. . . . Right after I started wearing jeans, somebody gave me my first Hawaiian shirt, and after that, I was gone; I got into a whole wild phase, and I learned to totally let go. Among other things, I learned to say 'For sure,' which Californians pronounce 'Furshirr.'"

Robin would soon make his first tentative experiments with drugs. He recalled the experience for *Playboy*:

Before coming to California, I hadn't even known what grass looked like. One of the first times I smoked it was on an astrological scavenger hunt—people who had the same astrological sign would pile into a bus and they'd drive all over the county searching for things like lost mandalas. The only problem I had with grass was that it got me real sleepy, so I didn't get into it and never have. At the time, though, there was a more important reason I didn't want to smoke it. I was on the cross-country running team, and I thought it would be bad for me. I thought that if I smoked grass, it would screw up my endurance. My hero then was Frank Shorter, who later won the Olympic marathon, and I grew a mustache so that I could look like him. Shorter's running mate was a guy named Jack Bachelor, and I and a teammate named Phil Russell used to fantasize that we were Frank and Jack. Our cross-country team would run up and down those beautiful northern California hills, and I remember going up a steep trail high on Mount Tamalpais and coming to the edge of it—and there, below us, was the fog sitting on Stinson Beach. That gave me a beautiful feeling, and I ran right down into the ocean. The other guys warned me not to go into the water, but it was too beautiful to resist. The moment I jumped in, both legs went out on me. It was like my body's saying, 'You use me so hard for an hour and then you do this to me? How's about if I cramp up both your legs? Think you'll remember not to jump in the water next time?'

I got stoned only once on a training run. I remember we came over a hill and there, in the middle of the trail, was this strange thing—a turkey vulture. Marin has a lot of them, and I thought, 'Well, it'll just move aside.' But when I got close, it went hssssss and spread its wings, and I turned to the rest of the guys and said, 'I knew this would happen if I got stoned. I can't deal with it!'

Robin kept his head screwed on long enough to graduate from Redwood High School. He decided to continue his education at Claremont Men's College near Los Angeles in southern California because the school had a good reputation for academics. Robin loved learning different languages; his ability to mimic the voices of others made him particularly adept at languages. Looking for way to use this skill, he played with aspirations for a career in the foreign service; he thought he might like to serve as a diplomat in an American embassy abroad or perhaps become an official in the U.S. State Department in Washington. And so, in the fall of 1970, he left home for college.

He soon forgot all about the foreign service. Instead, Robin discovered the theater.

Claremont Men's College offered a course on improvisational theater, and on a lark, Robin signed up for it. (He found the teacher attractive; that was the main reason he registered for the class, he later admitted.) He discovered that the class gave him a chance to make people laugh— and actually receive college credit for it.

"That was the trigger event because it was so easy for me. It was instantaneous," he told *Reader's Digest* in 1988. "I kind of exploded."

Soon Robin was spending more and more time around the Claremont theater and less and less time in classrooms. He failed most of his courses and was called home by his parents.

Oddly, though, he found his stern father supportive of his interest in the theater. Still, Robert Williams didn't like the idea of sending Robin to an expensive private college simply to learn how to act. No, Robin would transfer to Marin Junior College. That was fine with Robin; Marin Junior College had an excellent theater program.

While studying at Marin—Robin was an attentive student of Shakespearean drama—he also found himself hanging around San Francisco's comedy clubs. He especially liked improvisational comics (comedians who rarely work from a script or jokes prepared beforehand). These comedians more or less make up their comedy as they go

Robin Williams and his good friend Christopher Reeve attempt to hail a cab on the streets of New York. The two became very close while studying at the prestigious Julliard School in the early 1970s.

along, relying heavily on their quick wits and skills at mimicry to find humor in everyday objects, lampooning people in the audience, current events, or whatever happens to pop into their minds.

He made friends with members of The Committee, a local improvisational troupe, and learned many of their comedic techniques. Meanwhile, at Marin he acted and acted and acted, appearing in as many of the college's theatrical productions as he could. He kept up this nearly round-the-clock pace for more than two years.

In 1973 recruiters from New York's prestigious Julliard School stopped in San Francisco to audition prospective students for the school's acting program. Robin auditioned and was offered a full scholarship.

Before he left for Julliard, his father offered him a bit of advice. He told his son that he was a bit concerned that things wouldn't work out at Julliard, so he advised Robin to take up a trade. He suggested welding.

By that fall, Robin was in New York, studying under Julliard's master acting coaches, while he worked as a street mime in front of the Metropolitan Museum of Art whenever he needed money. At Julliard he met and struck up a lifelong friendship with another scared college kid who was far from home—Christopher Reeve.

Reeve recalled his early friendship with Robin Williams in a *Newsweek* interview in July 1986: "At first, he wasn't comfortable in New York. He was a California kid who wore karate clothes and a beret and was out of sync with people."

At Julliard, though, Christopher Reeve and Robin Williams made a pact: if either of them found himself in trouble later in life, the other would come to his aid. It was a promise that meant a lot to each man, a promise each aimed to keep.

But Christopher Reeve couldn't help Robin bail out of his current troubles at Julliard. Robin was under incredible pressure. He had been placed mostly in advanced classes at Julliard; his teachers were tough and they demanded the best from their students.

During one class, Robin was singled out by a teacher for ridicule. "You're mimicking people," the teacher complained. "Where is your own voice?"

Clearly, the teacher wanted Robin to bring more of himself to his work, to interpret the playwright's words and to bring his own emotions to the dialogue. Instead, Robin—the natural mimic—was merely imitating how other actors had played the role. His teacher had seen right through him.

That December 1973, just a few months after arriving at Julliard, Robin did not return home for the Christmas break. He was alone in the big city. His classes had not been going well. He missed his friends back in San Francisco. He missed the applause he got working with The

John Houseman, the head of Julliard's drama department, recognized Robin's talent and understood his weaknesses. He helped the struggling young student, and Robin came to look on the older actor as a mentor.

Committee. He was lonely and homesick, and he was scared that he didn't have what he needed to succeed in acting. Far from home, with little emotional support, he began to fall apart. Not surprisingly, Robin eventually suffered a mental breakdown.

"Except for my friendship with brother Reeve, that first year was rough, especially at Christmas time," Robin later admitted. "I couldn't afford to go back to California for the holiday, and it was the first cold, cold winter I'd experi-

enced in many years—and New York seemed unbearably
bleak and lonely. One day, I just started sobbing and
couldn't stop, and when I ran out of tears my body kept
going; it was like having emotional dry heaves. I went
through two days like that and finally hit rock bottom and
realized I had a choice: I could either tube out or level off
and relax. At that point, I became like a submarine on the
bottom that blows out some ballast and gets back up again.
. . . Once in a while, it's good to have a nervous breakdown. A little emotional housecleaning never hurt anybody. Once all my anxieties were behind me, the rest of
that year was easy."

Luckily, 1974 shaped up as a much brighter year. The
head of Julliard's drama department was John Houseman,
a veteran 70-year-old stage actor who had won an Academy Award playing a tough law school professor in the
movie *The Paper Chase.* Houseman immediately recognized, and understood, the problem with Robin. He had
him switched out of the advanced classes at Julliard and
into some less demanding courses. Robin responded to
Houseman and looked up to him. His next two years at Julliard were decidedly easier. He learned a lot about acting
in his years in New York.

But in the end he fell just short of getting his degree at
Julliard. Robin had fallen in love with a girl in San Francisco and he wanted to be with her. He was also anxious to
get on with his career, and most Julliard graduates were
hired by obscure road companies presenting small productions in small cities; Robin didn't have much interest in
waiting around to see what would break for him in New
York. So Robin quit Julliard.

It was 1976, and time to go home to San Francisco.

Almost overnight, Robin Williams became one of the most popular comedians in the country when the television show Mork and Mindy *debuted in September 1978. Viewers loved his zany antics, which were balanced out by his beautiful but down-to-earth costar Pam Dawber.*

3

INSTANT PANIC

JONATHAN WINTERS COULD take a telephone and find a dozen ways to make it funny. For example, he would play the part of a burglary victim: tied to a chair, totally immobile. Suddenly the phone rings. Winters would struggle over to the phone, his double chin rippling as he mimicked the act of a man bouncing in a chair on all four legs. The phone would ring and ring. Finally Winters arrived at the phone. He would crane his neck, grasping the receiver in his teeth, and then lay it on its side and press his ear to the handset. He would listen for a moment, his eyes would brighten, and then quite politely he would say, "Just a moment please."

And none of it was scripted. Winters had the ability to make up comedy as he went along, to improvise completely. He would tell reporters that his specialty was "winging it."

"Jonny works best out of instant panic," one of his writers told the *New York Times* in 1965. "Scripts inhibit him."

Winters could do much more, of course. He was a master of mimicry, able to lapse into the voices of dozens of eccentric characters he had developed over the years. Some of his characters included:

- Maudie Frickert, an 84-year-old grandmother who would grumble about most anything, but managed to keep her zest for life as well as her enthusiasm for chasing anything in pants. "Nobody writes to me because everybody is dead," Maudie would mutter.

- Zillionaire B. B. Bindlestiff: "I grow money trees. I plant poor people in the ground and money comes out."

- Moon-bound astronaut Sterling Studwell: "My wife keeps flashing those insurance premiums in my face and saying, 'When are you going? When are you going?'"

- A rich snob named Binky: "Bahbara and Oi ah racing to Nassau next week. Bahbara's sailing huh yacht and Oi'm sailing moine and whoever loses has to take the children for Christmas."

- A gun-toting ultraconservative: "I think every man, woman, and child should carry a .45 and a prayer book."

And on and on.

What's more, Winters didn't need much prompting to go into his act. He would gladly start doing improvisational comedy regardless of whether or not he was on stage. He just enjoyed performing.

"If he went into a store to buy a pair of shoes, he'd be on for the customers," a comedy writer told the *New York Times*. "If we got on an elevator with one other passenger aboard, immediately he'd be a surgeon who just operated on some big businessman on the 14th floor—right at the fellow's desk. He was on 24 hours a day."

Winters was a regular fixture on shows hosted by such early television icons as Garry Moore, Steve Allen, and Jack Paar. He was on television so often that viewers could see him performing on somebody's show virtually every night of the week. And Winters was on the big screen as

Comedian Jonathan Winters in character as Maudie Frickert. When Robin was growing up, Winters was one of his comic heroes.

well. He was featured in such mid-1960s comedy classics as *It's a Mad, Mad, Mad, Mad World; The Russians are Coming! The Russians are Coming!;* and *Eight on the Lam.*

Back home in Bloomfield Hills, Michigan, young Robin Williams had watched and learned. Jonathan Winters became his idol, and no other figure working in comedy influenced the young comic as much as this true pioneer of improvisational humor.

Robin arrived home from Julliard in 1976. He had left school before graduation because he missed his girlfriend in California, but things didn't work out with her. One month after leaving New York he found himself alone.

Meanwhile his stand-up comedy career was slowly getting started. In San Francisco he started playing the city's small comedy clubs while he worked at odd jobs on the side. One of those jobs was tending bar in a small nightclub, where he met Valerie Velardi, a young dance student working as a waitress. Robin approached Valerie using a phony French accent. Valerie could see right through the act, but she played along with the gag. The two of them became inseparable, and Valerie eventually took charge of Robin's career.

On stage, Robin brought his own version of "instant panic" to the improvisational comedy clubs of San Francisco. One of his favorite characters was an oily evangelist named the Rev. Ernest Lee Sincere. "Mama," he drawled to his audience one night, "I'm gonna lay my hands on your head and you will be able to sell insurance."

Another favorite character was Beverly Hills blues singer Benign Neglect: "Woke up the other day . . . ran out of Perrier," Robin warbled in a bluesy rhythm while he strummed an air guitar.

And then he would mimic celebrities. Aging actors George Jessel and Bette Davis were favorite targets; so was Mr. Rogers, the oh-so-polite and gentle children's TV host: "Let's put Mr. Hamster in the microwave oven, okay? Pop goes the weasel!"

The audience would roar, but Robin-as-Mr. Rogers was hardly finished. "Know why I did that, boys and girls?" Robin would ask in a perfect deadpan impersonation of Mr. Rogers, "because we're all going to die of radiation."

The jokes were earthy, the humor a bit out of the gutter—but Robin Williams had obviously simply updated Jonathan Winters's act for the younger, hipper audience of the mid-1970s. His comedy came out of his mouth in a constant, improvised stream, like a jazz musician playing riffs. For Robin, comedy was a compulsion. His explanation of this to *Newsweek* was simple: "I guess it's the 'Love me, love me' syndrome. I was lonely as a kid. [Being funny] was my way of making friends."

At this point in Robin's life, he may have been con-

trolled by his insecurities and neuroses, but Valerie was more practical. She knew how to channel Robin's amazing creative genius.

At Valerie's urging, the couple moved to Los Angeles because the comedy clubs in the southern California city were larger. Also, these clubs were frequented by producers and talent scouts who were constantly looking for talented young comedians to cast in TV shows and movies. Robin soon found himself playing to audiences in such important comedy meccas as the Comedy Store and Improvisation. It didn't take long for word to get out about this exciting young comic who consistently left his audiences in stitches.

One of the producers who caught Robin's act was George Schlatter, who had been responsible for producing

Robin and his wife Valerie at the fashionable New York club Studio 54. As Robin's career began taking off, he became more heavily involved in alcohol and drugs.

Beloved actor Jimmy Stewart shares a smile with Robin on the revival of Laugh-In. *Unfortunately, the show was not successful, and it was quickly canceled.*

Laugh-In, one of TV's classic comedies. The show appeared on network TV during the late 1960s and early 1970s, and featured a group of mostly unknown comics performing a smorgasbord of improvisational humor, slapstick jokes, and politically incorrect gags. Such phrases as "Sock it to me," "Verrrrry interesting," and "Look that up in your Funk and Wagnalls" entered the American lexicon, thanks to the cast of *Laugh-In*.

(The show was also the ticket to stardom for some of the *Laugh-In* cast members. Goldie Hawn's main job on the show—dancing in a bikini—was not particularly demanding, but she eventually went on to a movie career and an Academy Award. Movie actress Lily Tomlin also got her start on *Laugh-In*.)

The show eventually ran out of steam, though, and was canceled in the early 1970s. By 1977, Schlatter was pitching a revival of *Laugh-In* to the networks, and he was busily prowling the Los Angeles comedy clubs in search of talent. Robin was one of the first comedians Schlatter signed up for the show.

Unfortunately the revival of *Laugh-In* was far less successful than the original. The show lasted a handful of weeks and was quietly canceled. Still, Robin was on his way. Talent scouts liked his work on *Laugh-In* and cast him in a supporting role on *The Richard Pryor Show,* a comedy and variety program featuring the African-American comic whose humor dwelled mostly on race relations and life in urban ghettos. However, that show failed to find an audience and was soon canceled.

A third opportunity soon came along for Robin. *Happy Days* was an enormously successful situation comedy that had debuted in 1974 on the ABC television network. It showcased the lives of teenagers and their parents in 1950s Milwaukee. The show featured zany teen antics, plenty of rock 'n' roll music, and a lot of colorful and appealing characters. Perhaps the most popular of those characters was Arthur "Fonzie" Fonzarelli, a leather jacket–wearing Lothario with a broad, toothy smile, a greased-back duck-tail, and a good heart. By 1978, though, the writers were running out of ideas for "the Fonz." He had, after all, intimidated all the bad guys in Milwaukee, dated all the girls in town, and bailed his friends out of all their troubles.

So, wondered the show's writers, what if Fonzie met an alien from another planet? What if Fonzie gave the alien some tips on dating? What if the alien was really, really wacky?

Robin Williams was cast as the alien. He got himself the part when he was asked to sit down like an alien—and without pausing for a moment's thought sat on his head.

The alien was called Mork, and he was from the planet Ork. The *Happy Days* episodes with Mork were such a hit that the producers decided to base an entire series on the character.

The Fonz (Henry Winkler, right) shows Mork his signature move as Richie Cunningham (Ron Howard) looks on in a 1978 episode of Happy Days. *Robin made several appearances on the hit sitcom playing the wacky alien; interest in the character led ABC executives to create a spin-off series featuring Mork.*

In his autobiography *Wake Me When It's Funny,* TV producer Garry Marshall talked about how he came up with the concept for the new show. He related that it happened in the course of a few minutes during a short conversation with ABC network executives.

"How about a show about an alien who visits Earth, observes life here, and reports back his findings to his planet? We could call it the 'Mork Chronicles,'" Marshall told the executives.

But the network people didn't like the title.

Marshall changed course. He decided the show would need a female lead to costar with Robin Williams. "How about 'Mork and Melissa?'" Marshall suggested. "'Mork and Marlo'? 'Mark and Mindy'?"

"Mork and Mindy" seemed to roll off the tongue the best.

From there, Marshall conceived the plot: Mork would land in a small town—he suggested Boulder, Colorado, the first town to pop into Marshall's brain because his niece was going to college there. Mork would meet a young woman named Mindy. Each week, Mork would find himself entangled in a different crisis, and Mindy would help straighten things out. For the role of Mindy, Marshall suggested Pam Dawber, a young actress whose work Marshall admired. The network people agreed with the concept, and gave Marshall approval to produce the show.

When *Mork and Mindy* premiered in the fall of 1978, the American public immediately fell in love with Robin's character, and the show zoomed right to the top of the ratings. Mostly, all Robin had to do was play a wide-eyed, innocent stranger reacting to the curious customs of Earthlings. He let his talent take over and often strayed from the script by improvising gags right on the set as the cameras rolled. This made for some touchy nerves among the writers.

"When the series started, rumor was that we didn't have any writers," Marshall wrote in his book. "Robin Williams improvised it all, they said. Well, that wasn't the case. I know because I paid ten people to write scripts. The reason that the show worked well the first season was that the writers gave Robin a story structure or clothesline to hang his physical, hip, topical humor that set him apart from the rest. Mork represented your typical fish out of water. Each week people tuned in to see what zany thing he was going to discover about Earth. . . . It was a simple format, but made the most of Robin's talent. Yes, he ad-libbed, but he ad-libbed in character and many of the roads for his lines had already been paved by the writers."

There was also no arguing with the show's success. In its first season, *Mork and Mindy* was the third most-watched show on TV, with a final Nielsen rating of 28.6 (meaning that 28.6 percent of all TV sets in America that were on during the 8 to 8:30 P.M. time slot on Thursday nights were tuned to *Mork and Mindy*).

Robin's talent was also recognized elsewhere. Following the show's first season, he was nominated for an Emmy Award—TV's highest honor—for his role on *Mork and Mindy*, but he lost to veteran character actor Carroll O'Connor, who played Archie Bunker on the immensely popular *All in the Family*.

"This guy is going to be a superstar with or without this series," Dale McCrave, the cocreator of *Mork and Mindy*, told *Time* magazine in 1978. "He's such an overwhelming personality that he could never play a regular sitcom husband with a wife and kids. It would be a waste of his talent, a waste of his craziness."

Without a doubt, Robin Williams and *Mork and Mindy* were having an impact on American culture. Fans of the show greeted each other with the salutation "Na-noo, na-noo," the official way of saying "Hello" on Ork. Imitating Mork, fans tried to levitate eggs—with predictably disastrous results.

Mork also had a definite look. He dressed in baggy pants, colorful striped shirts, and rainbow suspenders. And despite Robin's improvisations with the scripts, the shows did have definite plots. Some of the early shows found Mork dodging the advances of a beautiful woman, fooling a newspaper reporter, unwittingly helping an escaped convict (Mork had a good heart and would help anyone in need), discovering the dating scene in a singles bar, and dealing with a neighborhood bully.

As for Robin and Valerie—who had married in June 1978, a few months before the show premiered—they found wealth and success. Robin was eventually paid $30,000 per episode for his work on *Mork and Mindy*. At first he and Valerie tried to live the lives of other young Californians; but one day, when they went roller-skating in Venice, a fashionable and seaside section of Los Angeles, Robin stopped to use a phone booth—and soon found himself surrounded by fans, gazing at him through the glass. "I felt like I was in the San Diego Zoo," he told *Time* in 1979. Robin could no longer blend into the California crowds.

Mork and Mindy returned for a second season and then a third and a fourth. Each year, though, the show's ratings slipped. Even Robin's talent couldn't keep the show at the top of the ratings; the original concept—a wide-eyed and innocent Mork learning about the curious customs of Planet Earth—was turning out to be old hat.

In fact there was nothing new about the concept. Another television show about an alien living on earth, *My Favorite Martian,* had been a hit more than 10 years before *Mork and Mindy* appeared. *Bewitched,* a show about a witch trying to fit in the mortal world, also pre-dated *Mork and Mindy* by several years. So audiences were used to extraterrestrials and their close cousins playing for gags on TV.

In one effort to save the show, the writers tried introducing sexy women into the plots. Some of the later shows had Mork cavorting with NFL cheerleaders as well as gorgeous girls from the planet Necrotron, but the public was growing weary of it all.

The producers even brought in Robin's idol, Jonathan Winters, to try to revive the sagging ratings. Winters played Mearth, a baby born to *Mork and Mindy* (they had gotten married in Episode 72). Granted, Winters was 55 years old in the final season of *Mork and Mindy*, but the plot explained that Orkian babies live their lives in reverse. Winters added a new element of craziness to the show. Pam Dawber reminisced to the *Allentown Morning Call,* "There was such brilliant improvisation that went on during the day, and to be allowed to watch these two geniuses work together . . . these two men with attention spans of 15 minutes each. Jonathan used to walk into scenes he wasn't written into. It was like doing a sitcom in an insane asylum."

Mork and Mindy was incredibly popular when it first appeared on television, but by its fourth season the show had become stale. Even the addition of Jonathan Winters to the cast could not help boost the show's sagging ratings; Mork and Mindy *was canceled in 1982.*

But despite the talents of both Robin and Winters, the show was on its deathbed, and nothing worked to reverse its decline in popularity. At the end of its fourth year, *Mork and Mindy* finished near the bottom of the ratings, and the show was canceled.

Years later, Pam Dawber spoke to a reporter about what went wrong on *Mork and Mindy*. Dawber explained that ABC had changed the time slot for the show so that it could compete against strong shows on competing networks and steal viewers. For example, after its first year near the top of the ratings on Thursday nights, ABC decided to switch the show to Sunday nights, where it would compete against *Archie Bunker's Place,* a spin-off of CBS's popular *All in the Family.*

When that didn't work, ABC juggled the time slot for *Mork and Mindy* again, Dawber said, and when that didn't work the show went for sex, featuring the cheerleaders and the aliens from Necrotron, among others.

"What they did was take all ABC's hit shows and spread them out to gun down shows on other networks. . . . We ended up splitting each other's audiences and it was a mistake," Dawber said.

Some people wondered why Robin put up with all the nonsense. After all, by now he was a star, and his opinions should have carried some weight. But Robin has never been the aggressive type. Besides, maybe he sensed that the time had come to go on to something new. Although it had been a great four-year run, Robin Williams was ready to focus on a career move to the big screen.

Olive Oyl (Shelly Duvall) gives her tough sailor beau a kiss in a scene from the movie musical Popeye. *Despite a good cast and experienced production team, the movie was a flop. However, Robin gained valuable experience, and his performance was generally well received.*

4

THE ELEPHANT
GOES DOWN

MOST PEOPLE ARE familiar with Popeye, the corncob pipe–chewing sailor with a taste for spinach and a deep belief that most wrongs can be corrected with a swift swing of his powerful fist—or, as Popeye might say, his "fisk."

Back in the 1920s the cartoonist E. C. Segar created the character Popeye, as well as his friends and foes—Olive Oyl, Bluto, Poopdeck Pappy, Swee' Pea, and Wimpy, among others. They first appeared in his comic strip, "Thimble Theatre." Later, animator Max Fleischer adapted Popeye to film, and by the 1960s most kids were growing up watching Popeye cartoons on television.

Robin Williams, who had virtually no big-screen experience at the time, was cast in the role of Popeye for a live-action film version that would be ready for the theaters in 1980. The movie was filmed on location in Malta, a rocky island in the Mediterranean Sea just off the coast of Italy. Director Robert Altman had decided that Malta would be the perfect place to simulate the town of Sweethaven, the ramshackle seaside village where most of the action in *Popeye* occurs.

The movie opens as Popeye rows a small boat into Sweethaven's harbor. He is met immediately by the Sweethaven tax collector, who demands Popeye pay up for docking his "sea craft."

"That ain't me sea crafk," croaks Robin in a perfect imitation of Popeye. "That's me dinghy."

In an interview with *Rolling Stone* in 1988, Robin explained that he had to "dub" the voice for Popeye twice. (Dubbing a film is the process where an actor has to go back and re-speak his part after he has already been filmed. Engineers then match the new spoken words with the action on celluloid.) "People couldn't understand what I was saying," Robin told Rolling Stone. "I sounded like a killer whale making rude noises in a wind tunnel."

Robin not only sounded just like Popeye, he also looked the part. The movie makeup people gave Robin cartoonishly large forearms and a blond dye-job for his hair. Throughout the film, the star kept one eye closed and walked with a definite Popeye shuffle as he muttered such vintage Popeye-isms as "I yam what I yam" and "Blow me down."

The movie soon finds Popeye renting a room in the Oyl family boardinghouse, where he learns that daughter Olive Oyl is to become engaged to Captain Bluto. Bluto is the town's evil overseer, running things for the mysterious, secretive, and wealthy Commodore.

Olive has decided to run out on her engagement. Popeye helps her escape and confides to Olive that he has really come to Sweethaven in search of his long-lost Poopdeck Pappy, whom he hasn't seen in 30 years. Together they discover an orphan. They decide to care for the baby and return to the boardinghouse, where they meet up with an enraged Bluto, who smashes Popeye through the Sweethaven boardwalk. Popeye, Olive Oyl, and Swee' Pea have a series of adventures that ends when Popeye rescues Olive from a giant octopus.

The film did not lack talent on either side of the camera.

Not only was Robin Williams electric, but the rail-thin Shelley Duvall was perfect as Olive Oyl. Other members of the cast were strong as well, and two minor players—Dennis Franz and Linda Hunt—went on to stardom, Franz as tough Detective Sipowicz on the television drama *NYPD Blue,* and Hunt in an Oscar-winning performance in the movie *The Year of Living Dangerously.*

Behind the cameras, the talent was top notch as well. Altman, the director, had made his mark in Hollywood as the director of the classic Korean War comedy *M*A*S*H.* Pop music icon Harry Nilsson supplied the songs for *Pop-eye.* Screenwriter Jules Feiffer was one of America's leading humorists, and he had a lot of fun with the dialogue.

Still, the critics gave the movie low marks. It was overproduced, they wrote, and the action was too helter-skelter; the musical numbers were forgettable, and the special effects were hardly dazzling.

"A game cast does its best with Jules Feiffer's unfunny script, Altman's cluttered staging, and some alleged songs by Harry Nilsson. Tune in to the old Max Fleischer cartoon instead; you'll be much better off," huffed film critic Leonard Maltin.

And yet, Robin Williams's role in *Popeye* undoubtedly established him as an important screen presence. He dominated every scene in which he played. Clearly, he was on his way to stardom.

For the record, *Popeye* wasn't actually Robin's first film. His first role in the movies had been the very forgettable *Can I Do It...Til I Need Glasses?* a low-budget bawdy farce released to the theaters in 1977. The 72-minute film is nothing more than a series of slapstick vignettes, some no more than a few seconds long, featuring the lowest type of bad jokes, toilet humor, and, for the most part, bad acting. Robin received only a few moments of screen time, appearing as a nerdy lawyer in a bow tie during a courtroom scene and later as a hillbilly with a toothache. The film had a brief run in some theaters, then

Robin gives a wacky stand-up performance in 1981. As a rising star in Hollywood, he kept himself busy, but he often succumbed to the temptation of cocaine and alcohol. He would later describe this out-of-control time of his life as "a madhouse."

dropped out of sight. It was the type of role a young actor in Hollywood finds himself accepting to earn a paycheck, make some contacts, and gain experience in front of the cameras.

Popeye was far more important to Robin Williams's career. Despite the film's bad reviews, Robin found himself a busy actor in Hollywood. Other movie scripts were arriving at his door. And he still found the time and desire to do improvisational stand-up at comedy clubs in Los Angeles.

Robin Williams was a bundle of energy in those days—but his world would soon come crashing down around him. He had developed a serious cocaine habit during his *Mork and Mindy* days. He was also drinking heavily, always looking for a party. For anybody with money and fame in Hollywood, the temptations were overwhelming.

"It was just a madhouse," Robin told an interviewer for *Newsweek* in 1986, "a time when you didn't want to stop. It got to the point where people said I'd go to the opening of an envelope. I felt like the top of a roulette wheel.

"With alcohol I blew up to forty pounds overweight—I was bloated."

Nevertheless, Robin told the magazine that he was careful not to use cocaine or alcohol before performing.

"One time I did," he admitted. "It's a nerve deadener. You totally withdraw into yourself. It basically removes your ability to make connections, your synapses are frying. . . . Now I realize it was the most boring time in the world. I was doing so many things, I could never really stop and enjoy one moment." In 1982, however, Robin was too deeply involved in drug and alcohol abuse to be able to understand this truth about his life.

A fellow comedian named John Belushi shared Robin's delusions about drug use. By 1982, Belushi was also at the top of his game. The rotund comedian had burst into the public eye seven years earlier as one of the featured players on the television revue *Saturday Night Live,* and he was soon making movies—*Animal House* and *The Blues Brothers* were both monster hits. And like Robin, Belushi also found himself heavily involved in the Hollywood party scene.

Robin Williams and John Belushi knew each other casually, and Robin admired Belushi's work. Both men claimed to have been inspired by the improvisational comedy of Jonathan Winters. They weren't good friends, but they were friendly.

According to an account of Belushi's death written by

John Belushi had risen to fame on the television show Saturday Night Live, *and become a cult figure thanks to hit movies like* Animal House *and* The Blues Brothers. *Although Robin and John were not close friends, they did know each other and would get together occasionally.*

author Bob Woodward in his book *Wired: The Short Life and Fast Times of John Belushi,* Robin found his way to Belushi's room in the Chateau Marmont Hotel in Hollywood early in the morning of March 2, 1982, after performing at an improvisational club. In the room he met Belushi and Belushi's friend, Cathy Smith.

Something about the scene made Robin uncomfortable. The room was tacky and messy, cluttered with dozens of opened wine bottles. He found Cathy Smith's mannerisms almost frightening, and he was disturbed to find Belushi so overweight and obviously depressed. Belushi seemed cross to have Robin see him in his current condition.

Belushi picked up a guitar and strummed a few chords, then put the guitar away. He got out some cocaine, and he and Robin both had some. Next, Belushi sat down and started nodding off. After about five seconds, however, he lifted his head.

"What's up?" Robin asked. "Are you okay?"

"Yeah," Belushi said. "Took a couple of ludes." (By that, Belushi meant he had already ingested two capsules of methaqualone, a heavy sedative usually administered to patients coming out of surgery. Drug abusers use methaqualone for its hypnotic effects.)

Robin felt sorry for Belushi, but the other man was obviously in a stupor, and Robin didn't know what he could do for him. After all, he didn't know the man all that well. If he had been closer to Belushi, he might have tried to talk to him about getting some help; between Belushi's depression and the drugs, the man obviously had a serious problem. As it was, though, Robin decided he might as well go home.

On his way out, though, he noticed a map of California hanging on the wall. "This is where I live," he told Belushi, pointing to a road on the map. "Give me a call, if you ever are in the area."

Belushi acknowledged the invitation and turned away— and Robin drove home. When he arrived, he told his wife Valerie about his brief meeting with Belushi and Cathy Smith. He described the woman with Belushi as "tough" and "scary."

Hours later, Belushi was dead, the victim of an overdose of cocaine and heroin administered by Cathy Smith. He was 33 years old, four years older than Robin.

Robin learned of Belushi's death the next day. "They told me on the set," Robin related to *Rolling Stone* magazine in 1982. "It was a sheer shock. The man, I thought, had the constitution of a bull. I certainly didn't know he was doing anything that would affect him in any way."

Pam Dawber also spoke to *Rolling Stone*. Here's how she remembered Robin's reaction to Belushi's death: "They hung out. Belushi was a guy who was a star and they could relate to each other, but they weren't close.

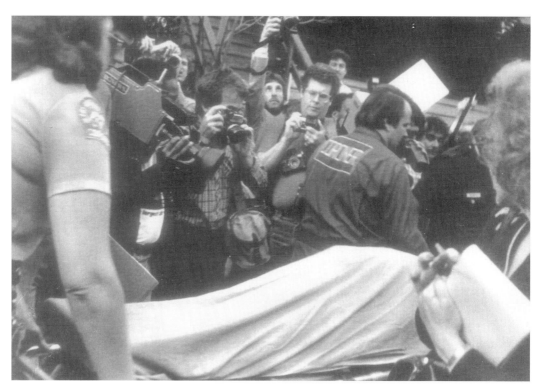

John Belushi's body is wheeled out of the Chateau Marmont on March 5, 1982. Belushi's death from a drug overdose was a wake-up call for Robin, who had shared cocaine with the comic actor the night before. Robin quit taking drugs and has remained clean.

Somebody told me to tell him [about Belushi's death]. Because they were afraid he'd fall apart. You never knew how he was going to take something, because he's so emotional. He was affected in a way, at first, that made it look as though he wasn't affected at all. He said, 'Wow, I was with him last night.'

"Then, as it absorbed, he became more and more devastated by it, because, suddenly, I think, he began to see the parallels—just what fast living can do. And also, somebody the same age, somebody you just saw that night, to then suddenly be dead. One day, I saw him in the studio, just standing, just thinking, and he said, 'Don't you worry, Dawbs. It'll never happen to me.'"

Belushi's death made international headlines. The Los Angeles police investigated it, and Robin even found himself testifying before a grand jury. He was absolved of any complicity in the case, but the death of John Belushi shook

Robin's world. It made him look deep inside himself to examine his own lifestyle.

"I was totally out of control for a while," Robin later admitted in an interview. "It was either fear or just a sheer wanting to run away from it all. I couldn't imagine living the way I used to live. I don't remember it as being anything except quick, with this series of people flashing through my life. Now people come up to me from the drug days and go, 'Hi, remember me?' And I'm going, 'No. . . .' It was kind of like my head was in a bell jar. I got crazier and crazier and then petered off."

Belushi's death was like a wake-up call for Robin. "It was like seeing an elephant go down," he recalled of Belushi. "Here's this guy who was a beast, who could do anything, and he's gone." And Robin answered the call immediately and thoroughly. He was completely off drugs within two months after Belushi's death, and he no longer touches alcohol or any other drug. "Cocaine is one of the most selfish drugs in the world," he says now. "[When you're on cocaine,] the world is as big as your nostril."

Robin's portrayal of Vladimir Ivanoff in the 1984 film Moscow in the Hudson *marked a turning point in his film career. The movie was very well regarded by critics and was Williams's first true box-office success.*

5

SNAIL ON THE GRILL

THE WORLD ACCORDING TO GARP was a runaway bestseller by author John Irving. It followed the life of writer T. S. Garp through a variety of humorous adventures, from his birth during World War II to his death at the hands of a radical feminist. Along the way, Irving's readers met a rich variety of characters, including a transsexual football player, a one-eared dog named Bonkers, and a unicycle-riding bear that lived in a broken-down Austrian boardinghouse.

None of that translated very well to the screen. The film version, starring Robin Williams, arrived in the theaters in 1982, and it received mixed reviews from the critics. "When the movie was over . . . all I could find to ask myself was: What . . . was that all about?" wrote film critic Roger Ebert, although Leonard Maltin called the film an "absorbing, sure-footed odyssey through vignettes of social observation, absurdist humor, satire, and melodrama; beautifully acted by all."

While Robin generally received good reviews for his acting in both *Popeye* and *Garp,* audiences stayed away from both movies. Neither film made the box-office sales it was expected to make. It was Robin's second starring role in a movie and, indeed, his second box-office failure. Robin's ability to draw audiences was starting to come into question.

Robin was concerned about the direction his career was taking. "You simply slip down the comedy food chain, that list of people who get scripts," Robin told a *Rolling Stone* interviewer. "From the top, there's Eddie Murphy and Bill [Murray] and Steve [Martin]. I guess on the next level there's Tom Hanks, myself, John Candy—there's a lot of us. It all kind of works that way."

With another failure at the box office, Robin said, "I'd go down a couple of notches. So you have to work your way back up again or do character parts—or you fall back and punt."

For Robin Williams, things would get worse before they got better. Certainly, it didn't help matters when he picked a flop for his next project. That film was *The Survivors,* which was released in 1983 and costarred the talented actor Walter Matthau. But again, audiences stayed away.

Finally, in 1984, Robin selected a project that would receive critical acclaim as well as box-office success: *Moscow on the Hudson.* He was cast by director Paul Mazursky to play Vladimir Ivanoff, a Russian saxophone player who defects to America from the former Soviet Union.

It was perhaps Robin's most challenging role to date. He prepared for the role of Vladimir Ivanoff by studying Russian extensively; indeed, the first third of the movie is staged in Moscow and most of the dialogue spoken by the characters is in Russian with English subtitles. In essence, Robin had to learn to speak Russian well enough to fool not only Americans but Russians as well. But Robin loved the challenge. And he finally had the chance to pursue his old love of foreign languages.

"Robin Williams . . . disappears so completely into his quirky, lovable, complicated character that he's quite plausible as a Russian," wrote film critic Roger Ebert.

However, Robin's successful portrayal of Vladimir is not very surprising. After all, Vladimir wasn't actually so very different from Robin himself. Vladimir is a character in search of freedom, the freedom to be true to himself. Defecting to America gives him a new taste of independence, but ultimately, no geographical location can provide anyone with total freedom. And while Vladimir longed to escape the restrictions of Russia, he finds himself an alien in the United States. He is lonely, longing for a place where he can fit in and be at home. These are also themes that have run through Robin Williams's life ever since he was a boy. And he too had some lonely times in New York City when he was attending Julliard, times when he longed simply to belong. Sometimes being free is not enough. We all need the connection to other people that assures us we are loved and accepted as we are.

Robin even saw a connection between *Moscow on the Hudson* and *Mork and Mindy*. He said, "Oddly, [playing Vladimir] was a little bit like Mork in that I was looking at the American culture from the outside."

The movie made money, too. It brought in more than $25 million—a modest success by Hollywood standards, but nevertheless a success. Robin went on to tell *Rolling Stone:* "I loved doing it. Immersing yourself into another language and culture is wonderful."

His work in *Moscow on the Hudson* proved to the critics that Robin could tackle roles that involved more than just light comedy. Soon after, when the opportunity came along to star in a public television production of *Seize the Day,* Robin quickly accepted. The production was based on a novel written by Pulitzer Prize–winning novelist Saul Bellow and centered on the character of Tommy Wilhelm, a failed salesman coming to terms with his life. *Seize the Day* was hardly light comedy.

Although Robin's movie career seemed back on track, his home life was another matter. Although he and Valerie had a son, Zachary, in 1984, their marriage had been

After the breakup of his marriage to Valerie, Robin remained close to his son; they try to spend a lot of quality time together. Here they are pictured with Robin's second wife, Marsha Garges.

unsteady for years and was now finally breaking up. They separated in 1986. Robin may have given up drugs, but there were other temptations.

"The thing is, it was never any one woman," Valerie Williams told *Rolling Stone.* "It was *lots* of women, and I'm not sure he had something intimately to do with them all. Most of it was just hanging out. He loves women and he likes hanging out with women."

Robin, devoted to his son Zachary, found himself separated from the boy. He tried to work through his troubles
by concentrating on the comedy club circuit, but he admitted that even his work on stage began to suffer.

"Things are rough," he told *Newsweek* in 1986. "Maybe
that's why there is a certain vehemence in my show; an
intensity. One of the foundations of your life is about to
change, and you're going, 'Yeah, let's play, ladies and
gentlemen, let's have a good time!'"

Give-and-take between Robin and the members of the
audience had always been a big part of his act, but now
Robin reported that he found himself interacting with
audience members less and less. He was afraid he would
snap at them.

"I'm just going to have to try and stay very calm. The
tendency is to overact at this point and just get crazy," he
told *Newsweek*. "It's a pretty raw time for me. I feel like a
snail on the grill."

His nonstop patter while playing Armed Forces Radio disk jockey Adrian Cronauer carried the 1987 film Good Morning, Vietnam *and earned Robin Williams his first Academy Award nomination.*

6

HAVING FUN

AS A MOVIE AND COMEDY star, Robin often found himself far from his San Francisco home. During the 1980s, Robin traveled to Malta to film *Popeye* and to Thailand for *Good Morning, Vietnam*. Other movies took him to locations throughout the United States. His comedy brought him to New York to appear as the guest host on TV's *Saturday Night Live* and to London, England, where he appeared at the Prince's Trust, a charity event organized by Prince Charles and Princess Diana. His schedule did not lend itself to maintaining close family ties.

Robin has two half brothers: Lauren Smith, who teaches high school physics in Memphis, Tennessee, and Todd Williams, who works for a wine company in northern California. In February 1988, Robin, Lauren, and Todd came together for a rare family reunion. But it was a sad occasion that had brought them together—the death of Robert Williams. Robin's father had lost his fight against cancer.

"I was here in San Francisco, and he died at home out in Tiburon," Robin told *Rolling Stone* in 1988. "So I was close. He had operations and chemotherapy. It's weird. Everyone always thinks of their dad as invincible, and in the end, here's this little, tiny creature, almost all bone. You have to say goodbye to him as this very frail being.

"At least he was at home and died very peacefully in his sleep. My mother thought he was still asleep. She came downstairs and kept trying to shake him. She called me that morning and said, 'Robin, your father's dead.' She was a little in shock, but she sounded happy in a certain way, if only because he went without pain."

Robin, Lauren, and Todd decided to scatter Robert Williams's ashes across the Pacific Ocean. "It was amazing," Robin told *Rolling Stone*. "It was sad but also cathartic and wonderful in the sense that it brought my two half brothers and me together. It kind of melded us closer as a family than we've ever been before. We've always been very separate.

"That day we gathered right on the sea in front of where my parents live. It was funny. At one point, I had poured the ashes out, and they're floating off into this mist, seagulls flying overhead. A truly serene moment. Then, I looked into the urn and said to my brother, 'There's still some ashes left, Todd. What do I do?' He said, 'It's Dad—he's holding on!' I thought, 'Yeah, you're right, he's hanging on.' He was an amazing man who had the courage not to impose limitations upon his sons, to literally say, 'I see you have something you want to do—do it.'"

Robin and his father might not have had the ideal relationship while Robin was growing up. And yet in the end, Robin was able to look back on his father's life and accept the gifts his father had given him: the gift of strength, the gift of courage to be himself, and yes, in his father's own way, the gift of love.

But other aspects of Robin's personal life were still very painful. By 1988 Robin and Valerie had been separated for two years. Zachary was living with his mother in a San Francisco apartment, but on the rare occasions when Robin was home, the boy would spend time with his father.

To cover his pain, Robin devoted himself to his work, especially a new venture—Comic Relief, a fundraising effort to help the homeless that Robin had put together with two friends, comedians Whoopi Goldberg and Billy Crystal.

The first Comic Relief show, which was carried live on the Home Box Office (HBO) cable network, played to a sold-out audience at the Universal Amphitheater in Los Angeles on March 29, 1986. It featured stand-up routines by 40 top comedians.

"The main thing is to make the funniest show possible, but not to jam it home or proselytize, or beg every five minutes . . . puhleeeeze," Williams told reporters before the show.

He added: "The only restriction is time. If you're going well, there's a tendency to want to go a little longer. If you're not doing well, there's a tendency . . . to want to go a little longer."

In addition to Robin, Billy, and Whoopi, the first cast for Comic Relief included such comedians and film actors as Steve Allen, Harry Anderson, Sid Caesar, Jerry Lewis, Madeline Kahn, John Candy, Bette Midler, David Steinberg, and Richard Dreyfuss, as well as performers from the satirical troupe, Firesign Theater. Also in the cast were Michael J. Fox, Estelle Getty, Mary Gross, Buddy Hackett, Pee Wee Herman, Michael Keaton, Eugene Levy, Howie Mandel, Pat Morita, Martin Mull, Minnie Pearl, Joe Piscopo, Gilda Radner, Carl Reiner, Rob Reiner, Dick Shawn, George Wendt, Henry Winkler, and Henny Youngman.

"Let's just say it's the greatest collection of funny people since Charlie Chaplin dined alone," quipped Billy Crystal.

Thanks to this first Comic Relief show, about 160 homeless people were hosted to a free meal and a comedy show at The Improvisation, a Los Angeles comedy nightclub. Also, the money raised by viewer pledges to

The crowd roars as Robin and Billy Crystal perform together at the first Comic Relief show in 1986. The show, which was also hosted by Whoopi Goldberg and featured a cast of great comedians, raised money to benefit the homeless.

Comic Relief was used for projects to help the homeless in 18 different cities.

Since 1986, seven Comic Relief shows have been produced, and Robin and the other performers have raised more than $35 million for agencies that assist homeless people.

Elsewhere on TV, viewers caught his act on a musical and comedy special starring comedienne Carol Burnett. Robin's appearance on the show garnered him an Emmy Award in 1987 for Outstanding Individual Performance in a Variety or Music Program.

Meanwhile Robin continued to find time for his own stand-up comedy work, constantly honing his craft as an improvisational comedian. In 1987 he appeared in a one-man show at the Metropolitan Opera in New York. Robin got things started by launching into a vocal rendition of composer Richard Wagner's dark and warlike "Ride of the Valkyries"—the same music that was played in the background during the helicopter attack in the movie *Apocalypse Now*. Robin, however, performed Wagner's aria in the voice of cartoon character Elmer Fudd. He went on to bounce from voice to voice, character to character. A small sampling:

- Roosevelt E. Roosevelt, an uncooperative weatherman: "You got a window? Open it."

- A baby in his mother's womb: "It sure is nice, except when she dances."

- A restaurant critic: "Here's a little advice: don't eat at a restaurant located next to a dog pound."

Newsweek described Robin as "a brain on constant spin cycle."

As for his movie work, Robin's performance in *Moscow on the Hudson* had opened producers' eyes. The role helped launch him into important films with socially relevant themes.

The first of those films was *Good Morning, Vietnam*, a comedy-drama loosely based on the life of Adrian Cronauer, who worked as a disc jockey for Armed Forces Radio in Saigon, entertaining American soldiers during the Vietnam War. Cronauer was an early version of today's "shock jocks" who specialize in outrageous humor. The title of the movie was drawn from Cronauer's signature sign-on every morning as he opened his show: "Good Morning, Vietnam!" he would shout into the microphone. The film, released in 1987, was an immediate smash hit.

Robin's next important film was *Dead Poets Society*. In this film he played a private school English teacher named John Keating, who literally throws the book away in order to teach his young students both a love of literature and to make the most of every day. One of his unorthodox methods of teaching includes encouraging his students to meet secretly in a cave to read poetry aloud to each other. The students follow this suggestion and form a "Dead Poets Society." The film, which was released in 1989, dealt with many deep social issues, including teenage suicide. Critics praised Robin's performance as one of his strongest.

Two years later, *The Fisher King* was released. In this movie Robin played Parry, a mentally unstable man who has been wandering aimlessly since his wife suffered a violent death. He meets up with Jack, a former shock jock whose rantings on the radio encouraged a deranged man to walk into a restaurant and open fire on the patrons. Seven people died in the incident, including Parry's wife. Parry and Jack form a friendship, despite Jack's guilt, and the movie ends on a note of triumph and hope.

Those three films mark milestones in the career of Robin Williams because he earned Academy Award nominations for best actor for each of them. In all three cases, however, he fell short of winning the award. Nevertheless, his strong work on the screen left little chance that he would be relegated to lesser films, which he had feared after some of his earlier movies had floundered at the box office.

These were not the only quality films Robin appeared in during this period, however. He had received rave reviews for his performances in two 1990 hits: *Cadillac Man* ("Williams is terrific, as usual, playing an aggressive car salesman who may lose his job, his mistress, his other girlfriend, his Mafioso protector, and his daughter all during one eventful weekend," wrote critic Leonard Maltin) and *Awakenings* ("Powerfully affecting true-life story of a painfully shy research doctor who takes a job at a Bronx hospital's chronic care ward in 1969—and discovers that his comatose patients still have life inside them. Williams is superb as the doctor," Maltin commented). He also costarred in Stephen Spielberg's updated version of the Peter Pan story, *Hook,* along with a great cast that included Dustin Hoffman, Julia Roberts, and Bob Hoskins. However, the 1991 film was poorly received by critics, and was

only modestly successful at the box office.

Robin also found himself taking part in a piece of television history. On May 22, 1992, Johnny Carson—then the host of *The Tonight Show,* which now features Jay Leno—intended to retire after some 30 years as the star of late-night TV. Carson decided that his last show would be a sentimental journey he would share with his many friends, whom he invited to *The Tonight Show* studio in Burbank, California. But for his next-to-last show, Carson wanted to go out with some real electricity. So he booked two guests for that night: singer Bette Midler and Robin Williams. Robin appeared early in the show, and for nearly the next hour kept Carson, as well as the *The Tonight Show* audience, in stitches with his improvisational humor.

Clearly Robin's career had found a new direction. And people who knew Robin were convinced his career had been given that new direction by Marsha Garges, the

Playing a young English professor at a prep school, Robin tells his class to "seize the day" and make every moment count. Dead Poets Society *became one of the biggest hits of 1989, and earned Williams a second Academy Award nomination as best actor.*

Williams teamed up with Jeff Bridges in the 1991 hit The Fisher King. *The film drew critical praise—"unusual and absorbing, both comic and tender, this [film] takes the viewer on quite a journey," wrote one reviewer—and Robin was nominated for an Academy Award for the third time.*

woman who became his second wife.

"Marsha is Robin's anchor," Pam Dawber told *People Weekly* in 1988. "She's reality. Ground zero. She's very sane, and that's what he needs. She's incredibly loving, too. And protective. She knows who is bad for him and who is good, and she helps keep the good relationships going."

Marsha Garges grew up in Milwaukee, Wisconsin. She aspired to be an artist but eventually found herself working in a bank and then as a waitress. She also endured two bad marriages.

Marsha and Robin met in 1984, when Marsha was hired by Valerie Williams to be a nanny for Zachary. It was a difficult period for Robin and Valerie; their marriage was very much on the rocks, and two years later they separated. Robin asked Marsha to remain with him, working as a secretary and part-time nanny for Zachary during the times when the boy would stay with his father. Marsha agreed and soon became an important part of Robin's life. When Robin had to spend several weeks in Thailand filming scenes for *Good Morning, Vietnam*, Marsha accompanied him, proving herself a valuable assistant.

"She was the hardest working person on the set," Mark Johnson, the producer of *Good Morning, Vietnam*, told *People Weekly.* "She was there for him twenty-four hours a day."

They were married on April 30, 1989, in Lake Tahoe, a resort city in Nevada.

Marsha did bring stability to Robin's life and career, but he found himself enduring some embarrassments left over from his former hedonistic life. In 1988, Tish Carter, a former girlfriend, filed a lawsuit against Robin, claiming that he had infected her with herpes, a sexually transmitted disease. The ex-girlfriend asked a judge to reward her $6 million for the suffering she had to endure as a herpes patient.

(Herpes is no insignificant disease—as many as 80 million Americans suffer from the sores and rashes that accompany the virus. There is no known cure, although drugs are available to minimize occurrences of the uncomfortable and itchy symptoms that appear on the genitals of men and women who suffer from the disease. Although herpes is at its most contagious when the blister-like sores are present on the skin, people who carry the virus can pass it along at any time they have physical—usually, sexual—contact with other people.)

The lawsuit against Robin led to a lengthy legal fight. A few months after the woman filed the case against him, Robin filed his own countersuit against his former girlfriend. The case dragged on for nearly five years. Finally, as it appeared headed for trial in a California courtroom, Robin decided to settle out of court with the woman. The terms of the settlement were never announced; all the

Friends credited Marsha Garges, Robin's second wife, with helping to bring balance to his personal life. The couple was married in 1989.

parties agreed to keep the matter a secret.

If his fans wondered how the unpleasant business of such a lawsuit would affect Robin's career, they needed only to look at the box-office receipts for *Aladdin*. This animated movie by Walt Disney Studios eventually earned $217 million. The story was typical for a Disney animation: a young hero and heroine overcome evil to triumph in the end. Along the way they meet up with magical creatures, who provide the comic relief. But *Aladdin* was a bit different from any other Disney movie because this time, the comic relief—in the form of a big blue Genie—took over the movie. Robin Williams, of course, was the Genie's voice.

The Genie makes his entrance into the movie about a third of the way through the narrative. From that point on, Robin's voice characterization dominates the film. Clearly, a lot of his dialogue was improvised. In the span of a few seconds, the Genie lapses into a dozen different voices, mimicking Groucho Marx, Tarzan, William F. Buckley, Peter Lorre, Robert De Niro, Arnold Schwarzenegger, a street punk ("Yo, rug man . . . haven't seen you in a few millennium. Gimme some tassel."), and Ed Sullivan.

As a result, the movie has a faster, looser feel to it than any other Disney movie. The Genie even pokes fun at Disney itself, with jokes about Pinocchio and Sebastian the crab (from *The Little Mermaid*). In large part, Robin Williams set the tone for the entire movie.

Not only did Robin provide the voice of the Genie, but the animators readily conceded that he also inspired the artwork. Just as Robin Williams's stand-up routine has always involved his mimicking the voices of a stream of different characters, the Genie does the same—except when the Genie imitates Arnold Schwarzennegger or Ethel Merman, he not only sounds like them, he *looks* like them. Eric Goldberg, the Genie's animator, had to draw 60 different characters to keep pace with Robin.

And when the Genie wasn't mimicking anyone, he looked something like Robin. "If you look hard, you can see Robin in the Genie's eyes, nose, and mouth," Eric Goldberg told reporters. Goldberg also said that when Robin was doing the voice in the studio, the animators were unsure they could keep up with him. "When we got Robin on the soundstage the first time, out came Peter Lorre, Groucho Marx, and Ed Sullivan," said Goldberg. "We knew it would be a crying shame not to include Robin's improvisations in the movie. Most of those people that Robin mentioned were people I had never drawn or animated before. It was the kind of thing where each new one turned out to be another challenge."

Obviously Robin was having fun. And Robin's fun added a unique, spontaneous quality to *Aladdin* that brought him admiration from both critics and fans. As a result his professional life was speeding forward, keeping pace with the new happiness he had found in his personal life.

It took four hours for makeup artists to transform Robin into the elderly but spirited nanny Eugenia Doubtfire. Mrs. Doubtfire *was an immediate hit when it was released in 1993.*

7

A HIP OLD LADY

COMEDIAN BILLY CRYSTAL had known Robin Williams when Robin was heavily into drugs—but back then they didn't have much in common. Billy Crystal thinks of himself as a family man, and Robin's wild lifestyle didn't appeal to him. The first time Billy and Robin really connected was when Robin's son Zachary was a baby. "He was crying, and Robin was having a little trouble quieting him down," Billy told *Us* magazine. "So I showed him a technique from Dr. Spock—massaging the back of the baby's skull. I remember we talked about babies that night—it wasn't like frantic comics trying to top each other." After Robin's marriage to Marsha, as his life became still more stable, his friendship with Billy Crystal became even deeper.

Says Billy, "Since Marsha and he got married, I don't know if he's quieted down—he's just himself better." Obviously, marriage to Marsha has been good for Robin.

Some people believe that Marsha took a weak man and saved his life with her own strength. However, Robin had already begun to change his life even before his relationship with her began. After John

Belushi's death and the birth of his son Zachary, Robin made changes in his life—and then never looked back.

Marsha Williams acknowledges Robin's strength. She told *Us*, "Was he troubled? Absolutely. Was he actually in danger? I don't think so. Robin has a great sense of self-preservation." Robin says of himself that he was like a child who is waiting for someone to draw the line; he was hoping that someone would come along and tell him his behavior had gone too far and it was time to stop. But in the end, he drew his own line. And he never crossed it again.

He and Marsha make a good team. Marsha is a practical, take-charge person who helped to focus Robin's creative energy. Their partnership works well not only emotionally but also professionally.

Robin and Marsha made big plans together on all the levels of their life. They started their own family—daughter Zelda was born in 1989; son Cody would follow two years later. Next the couple formed Blue Wolf Productions. With the establishment of the company, Robin could not only star in many of his movies but also have a hand in how they were produced—meaning that he controlled who was selected to direct, what actors were picked to play other roles, how much money was spent on the film, what cities were picked to do the filming, and the thousand other details associated with a Hollywood production. Robin now had a big say in all that, and as president of Blue Wolf Productions, Marsha Williams did as well. For their first production, Marsha and Robin picked a script based on *Alias Madame Doubtfire,* a popular children's novel by Anne Fine.

In the movie, Robin's character, an underachieving actor named Daniel Hillard, disguises himself as a nanny—Mrs. Doubtfire—in order to take care of his children after he and his wife Miranda separate. It took some Hollywood magic to turn Robin into a woman. On screen, Daniel is able to slap on the mask, jump into a dress, throw on a wig,

Marsha, Robin, and their daughter Zelda attend a special performance of Beauty and the Beast. *Marsha and Robin started a family shortly after their marriage; they also have a son, Cody.*

and materialize as Mrs. Doubtfire in a matter of seconds. In reality, it took four hours of preparation in the makeup chair for Robin to be transformed into the character before the day's filming could commence. Not since his days on the *Popeye* set had Robin been required to undergo such extensive physical preparation for a role.

Mrs. Doubtfire treats the audience to vintage Robin Williams. In one scene featuring short, snappy camera cuts, he impersonates a Martian, a Russian, Groucho Marx, Chico Marx, Sean Connery (playing James Bond),

Ronald Reagan, character actor Walter Brennan, Humphrey Bogart, a man from India, and even a hot dog.

As a part of the movie's plot, Mrs. Doubtfire becomes the star of a new children's show. "I'm a hip old lady . . . hip hop, bebop, dance till ya drop and yo yo I make a wicked cup of cocoa," she announces to her audience on the first show.

Although *Mrs. Doubtfire* is a lighthearted movie with lots of laughs—including the scenes when Robin's character's double life is finally discovered—the movie does not have a completely happy ending. Daniel and Miranda Hillard do not reconcile, and the family must deal with the pain of separation.

As Daniel collects the children for his first outing with them after his double life is found out, the camera pans to the TV set. On screen, Daniel is in character as Mrs. Doubtfire on her television show, and reads a letter from a young viewer. It seems the little girl feels responsible because her parents are getting divorced. "Don't blame yourself," Mrs. Doubtfire says. "Just because they don't love each other anymore doesn't mean they don't love you."

This is the final scene of the film. Studio executives had pressured Marsha and Robin to change the ending—to reunite Daniel and Miranda at the close of the movie. Marsha and Robin resisted.

"Ninety percent of parents who separate don't get back together again," the movie's director, Chris Columbus, told *The New Yorker* in 1993. "We don't want our audiences to see a dishonest film. We didn't set out to make *The Parent Trap*. We're going to protect Mrs. Doubtfire. We're keeping it honest."

Perhaps because of his own experience, Robin felt strongly that *Mrs. Doubtfire* needed its "honest" ending, rather than a feel-good, sugarcoated conclusion. And apparently a lot of people saw things Robin's way. *Mrs. Doubtfire* earned nearly $220 million at the box office, making it Robin's most successful movie to date.

Still, there were dissenters. Former Vice President Dan Quayle questioned the message *Mrs. Doubtfire* sent out to families: that a mother and father could live apart and still maintain a functional, loving family. It was a complaint similar to the criticism he had leveled toward the producers of the TV show *Murphy Brown* in 1992, when the title character of the sitcom, a single woman, decided to have a baby and raise the child in a home without a father.

"The ideal situation for our children is to be born and raised in an intact family," Quayle said.

However, despite Quayle's criticism, family love stands out as an important part of *Mrs. Doubtfire,* even if the movie's family is not "intact." "We want to show that a family forms in any number of combinations," Chris Columbus asserted, "and that as long as there is love, there is family." As an affirmation of family love, the filmmakers had their own families—mothers, fathers, children, grandparents, and even dogs—on the set every day, so that families could be together for meal breaks and in the screening rooms.

Robin had a deeply personal response to the movie's message. "This movie is about real family values," he told *New York* magazine in 1993. "After a divorce, how many fathers just give up? The tendency is to say, 'I love my son,' and then just pull away. If you're lucky, the father becomes an uncle. But the weird thing is, he needs his kids as much as they need him."

Robin knew what he was talking about. After all, he had been through a divorce from Valerie, and that had meant separation from his son Zachary. He understood that when you are a parent, almost all of your actions have consequences that affect your children. And like his character in *Mrs. Doubtfire,* he could relate to a father's insecurities and longing for his children after the breakup of a marriage.

Speaking about his son Zachary, Robin told *Rolling Stone,* "I've learned to have the security not to worry that he will love me, as long as I keep the connection strong enough. I've learned not to try to force love. You can't. All you can do is try to set up a world for him that's safe and stable enough to make him happy. I want to protect him and shield him. . . . I want him to have his own life."

Robin appears to have been successful at making his son feel secure and loved. However, Robin knows that all children whose parents are divorced go through a time of serious adjustment. His son Zachary divides his time between Robin and Marsha's home and his home with his mother. Says Robin, "He sometimes gets confused and calls someone by the wrong name. But we have a good custody agreement, so he comes and goes freely. He knows exactly how many days he's here and how many days he's there. Children at his age do not want to deal with the anger and the volatility or whatever would develop. As long as things are peaceable, he's fine switching back and forth."

Robin's next film was another hit. *Jumanji,* a special-effects laden fantasy about a boy trapped in a board game, earned more than $100 million at the box office in 1995. The movie echoes Robin's own childhood, for the lonely teenage hero is a lot like Robin was at the same age. Robin told the *Allentown Morning Call,* "I grew up in a giant house like the one in the movie. . . . There were no kids around. And my father was very strict and very elegant, a bit like the dad in the movie. I remember being in seventh grade, feeling fat, small, and white. I was called 'leprechaun' and 'dwarf.'" Like Robin, the hero of *Jumanji* is also picked on and ridiculed by his peers.

Robin pushed his talent in new directions as well. He agreed to play a small role in actor-director Kenneth Branagh's four-hour film of *Hamlet.* It was essentially Robin's first Shakespearean role since his Julliard days. In the film, which was released in 1996, he plays Osric, who referees the duel between Hamlet and Laertes. (Osric, by the way, takes a sword in the stomach during the duel and

eventually dies, the first time Robin played a death scene on film.)

Another 1996 film was the hit *The Birdcage,* a remake of the French farce *La Cage aux Folles.* The film is about a gay couple—Armand and Albert—that must pass as straight when Albert's son brings home his fiancée, the daughter of a conservative senator. To pull off the ruse, Albert must dress as a woman. Robin had originally been slated to play Albert, but he insisted on the role of Armand because he had had enough of cross-dressing in *Mrs. Doubtfire.* The next year, Robin starred in *Flubber,* a remake of the classic Disney hit *The Absent Minded Professor,* which raked in $92 million.

One of Robin's big hits of the mid-1990s was The Birdcage, *an Americanized version of the French farce* La Cage aux Folles. *The movie thrust his costar, Nathan Lane (left) into stardom; other cast members included Gene Hackman, Dianne Wiest, and Christine Baranski.*

Released in time for the 1997 holiday season, Flubber *became one of Robin Williams's biggest hits. A remake of the 1961 Disney hit* The Absent Minded Professor, Flubber *earned more than $90 million.*

These were good times for Robin Williams. His drug problems were behind him. His family life had stabilized. His movies were big hits. However, not everything was perfect in Robin's life.

His friend from Julliard, Christopher Reeve, had also found success in Hollywood. Reeve went on to play Superman in a string of movies based on the famed comic book hero. Although he will forever be identified as the "Man of Steel," Reeve eventually stepped away from the part, preferring instead to find other roles that would challenge his acting talents.

Away from the cameras, Reeve had become an avid competitor on the equestrian circuit, riding specially trained horses over courses that include such obstacles as fence gates, pools of water, and other obstructions. On May 27, 1995, Reeve was competing in an equestrian event in Virginia when his horse, Buck, refused to leap over a gate. The horse stopped suddenly, throwing Reeve forward. He landed on his head, snapping two bones in his neck. He was flown to a nearby hospital, where he spent the next five days fading in and out of consciousness. Doctors gave him a 50-50 chance of living. As he regained his senses, he noticed that a thick-set figure dressed in a white doctor's coat had wandered into his room. Suddenly, the doctor said, in a heavy Russian accent, "At your cervix!"

It was Robin. He was at Reeve's bedside . . . doing improvisational comedy! Robin had flown to Virginia to be with his friend. After all, they had made a pact back in their Julliard days that if either of them were ever in need, the other would come to his aid.

"My first reaction was that either I was on way too many drugs or I was in fact brain damaged. But it was Robin Williams. He and his wife, Marsha, had materialized from who knows where," Reeve recalled in his 1998 autobiography, *Still Me*. Reeve added: "For the first time since my accident, I laughed. My old friend had helped me know that somehow I was going to be okay." Robin's comedy routine helped Reeve realize that although his life would be very different from here on, full of immense challenges, he could still find the joy in life. Robin had given him back the gift of laughter.

Reeve's old friend would eventually do something else for him as well. The tall, robust actor who played the Man of Steel has never recovered from his injuries. Although Christopher Reeve holds onto his hope that through rehabilitation and operations he will one day regain full use of his arms and legs, he remains confined to a wheelchair, completely paralyzed. He breathes through a tube inserted in his throat and needs round-the-clock nursing care.

Christopher Reeve, like most Americans, receives his health care through an insurance company that places limits on how much it will pay for a patient's care. Reeve suffered an injury that required months of hospitalization,

Robin Williams and his friend Christopher Reeve. After a riding accident left Reeve paralyzed and confined to a wheelchair, Robin kept his Julliard promise. He has spent hundreds of thousands of dollars to help pay Reeve's medical bills.

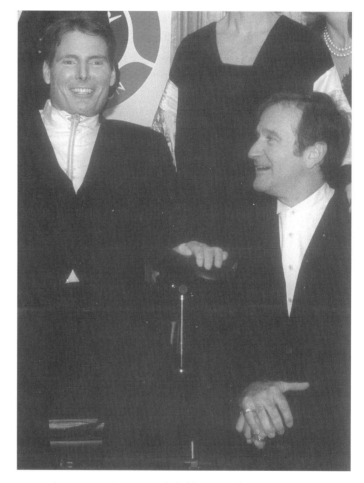

extensive operations, and daily care by nurses, and his health insurance eventually ran out. That's where Robin stepped in. He promised to pay for his friend's medical care for as long as he would need it—a sum that is estimated to be $400,000 a year.

That generosity was cited in a speech by Senator Paul Simon of Illinois. "Actor Robin Williams has pledged to pay Christopher Reeve's medical bills when the paralyzed actor's health insurance runs out," Simon said. "Williams and Reeve made a pact more than twenty years ago, when both were attending Julliard, that if either made it in show business, he'd help the other in time of crisis."

Simon used the Reeve-Williams pact to point out that most disabled Americans do not have wealthy friends to come to their aid when their health benefits run out. Indeed, throughout the 1990s, Congress has been unable to come up with a plan to ensure all ill or disabled Americans receive the care they need, regardless of the cost. Nevertheless, Simon said, "I applaud what Robin Williams is doing."

Robin has kept the vow he made all those years ago to Reeve.

Will (Matt Damon) and Sean (Robin Williams) interact in a scene from Good Will Hunting.

8

THE OPEN
ROAD AHEAD

WHILE ROBIN HAD PLAYED dramatic roles before, rarely had he ever gone through an entire film or play without falling back on comedy. Robin had even managed to inject some slapstick humor into the role of Estragon in the dark play *Waiting for Godot,* Samuel Beckett's classic drama about lost souls. Robin played Estragon for 11 weeks at Lincoln Center in New York in 1988. (The playwright was not amused; adding humor to the serious character of Estragon enraged Beckett.)

Good Will Hunting, however, was not played for laughs. Although the film does have its light moments, none of them involve Robin. His character, psychotherapist Sean Maguire, is reserved; after seeing the film, one can't imagine the intense Maguire exploding in a series of improvisational gags and voices. No, Sean Maguire is a troubled soul, as troubled as Will Hunting, the protagonist of the film.

The movie unfolds on the campus of the Massachusetts Institute of Technology (MIT), perhaps the nation's most elite school for students of engineering, mathematics, and the sciences. Professor Gerald

Lambeau, a top MIT mathematics professor, writes an equation on the blackboard outside his classroom that he challenges his students to answer. He cautions them that it is likely to take them the entire semester to come up with the answer. Soon, Will Hunting, who works at the school as a janitor, sees the problem. He studies it for a few moments, tries to work out the equation at home, and the next day chalks in the answer. No one has seen him do it, and suddenly there is a great mystery on campus: who is the mathematical genius who overnight solved a problem that ordinarily should have taken months?

Eventually, Lambeau tracks Will down, finding out through the building superintendent that Will got the janitor's job through his parole officer. Will has a criminal record for fighting, car theft, and other crimes. He is an orphan, having been raised in a series of foster homes, where he underwent physical abuse (he has scars on his body from cigarette burns and stab wounds). Lambeau also finds out that Will is looking at a lengthy prison sentence for punching a policeman. So he gets the judge to release Will into his custody, as long as Will agrees to work with the MIT mathematicians and undergo psychiatric counseling.

Will is at first hostile to the therapists. One calls him a "raving lunatic" while another mutters to Lambeau that Will "is a waste of my time." Finally, Lambeau approaches an old friend—Sean Maguire, a professor at a local community college. This is the audience's first view of Robin Williams in the film; he wears a beard streaked with gray and looks professorial behind wire-rimmed glasses.

The first meeting between Will and Sean doesn't go well. Will wanders around Sean's office, criticizing the books he sees on shelves. He sees a small oil painting on the wall—a man in a rowboat—that was painted by Sean. He makes fun of the painting and then insults Sean's wife.

Suddenly, Sean starts choking Will and warns him never to insult his wife again. Will nods his head and leaves.

Wearing a red foam nose, in the manner of his character from Patch Adams, *Robin places his hands in wet cement outside the Hollywood landmark Mann's Chinese Theater on December 22, 1998.*

Will's second meeting with Sean doesn't go well, either. This meeting is in a park, as the two men sit on a bench by a lake. It is during this meeting that the audience discovers that Sean has a side as dark as Will's. His wife died after a long fight with cancer, and Sean had fought in Vietnam, where his best friend died in his arms; like Will, he too comes from a rough south Boston neighborhood.

This scene, which runs some four minutes, probably won the Academy Award for Robin Williams. During the scene, the camera never leaves Robin's face: he exudes emotions of remorse, pity, and hate merely by raising or lowering his voice and by using slight facial expressions— a half-smile here, a frown there, a furrowed forehead.

There is no question, however, that Will, as played by Matt Damon, is the lead character in *Good Will Hunting* and that Sean is a supporting character. Williams has few scenes without Damon in the film, and the producers were justified in submitting Robin's nomination to the Academy Awards competition in the Supporting Actor category rather than as a lead actor. However, Robin's name does appear first in the credits—a nod by the filmmakers, perhaps, to the fact that the name of Robin Williams above the title means big box-office receipts.

His Oscar-winning performance in *Good Will Hunting* could certainly have capped Robin's career. But he has gone on to appear in other, equally demanding roles. Robin appeared in the title role of *Patch Adams,* a film about a flamboyant doctor who treats his young patients with humor. *What Dreams May Come,* the story of a man who searches for his wife in the afterworld, is another of Robin's movies, as well as *Jakob the Liar,* which tells the tale of a man who shelters a young girl in the Warsaw ghetto during World War II. At the end of 1999, his film *Bicentennial Man* was released. Robin has also been mentioned as a likely candidate to play the Mad Hatter in yet another sequel to *Batman.* To date his career has covered live comedy, work in TV, and appearances in more than 30

In one of Robin's more recent films, Jakob the Liar, *he plays a Jewish cafe owner in Nazi-occupied Poland during World War II. He keeps hope alive among his neighbors in the ghetto by making up false news stories about Allied successes in the war against Germany.*

feature films. The public's desire for Robin Williams never seems satisfied.

Between movies, Robin, Marsha, and their children relax in their elegant Mediterranean-style mansion in San Francisco, far from the glitter, glamour, and temptations of Hollywood. The mansion has a sweeping view of the Pacific Ocean and the Golden Gate Bridge.

Inside, the house is packed with both art and toys. Some of the toys belong to the children of course, but some belong to Robin. He has his own room filled with every imaginable sort of action figure. In the living room, alongside miniature, child-size couches, are cages of rabbits and iguanas. The dining room table is covered with science projects; Robin's desk holds both books and computer games that he shares with Zach. For Robin, his home is a sanctuary, a playhouse, and a museum, all at the same time. The house seems to express the peace and stability, as well as the creativity and childlike sense of fun that Robin has achieved in recent years.

Robin's family is a huge part of his current happiness. Despite his separation from his first wife, he has managed to stay close to his son Zachary. He admits that staying connected with Zach has not always been easy, and he gives Marsha credit for helping him to maintain that relationship. Marsha, Robin told *New York,* "reminded me that no matter what angers I had, I had to put Zachary first. Slowly but surely, it started to sink in. And we made it through."

As Zach moves into the teenage years, Robin faces the bittersweet pain of watching his son become a man. He was relieved to see that when Zach went to his first formal dance, he dressed in camouflage and Dr. Martens boots instead of a tuxedo; Zach is, after all, Robin's son! But when Zach's date came to pick him up, Robin told *Us* magazine, "It was like a wonderful kind of sad but happy moment, because as I walked away, they hugged and kissed, and it was like, 'This is it. It begins.'"

Robin Williams has had many beginnings in his life. As a teenager, he had a new beginning when his family moved from the proper atmosphere of suburban Michigan to the far freer world of northern California. Then came another new beginning—his years at Julliard in New York City. Next came his return to California, his marriage to Valerie, his years doing comedy clubs—which were followed with yet another new start when Robin moved from comedy clubs to television for *Mork and Mindy.* These were

Robin's wild years of drugs and sex—but luckily for Robin, his life did not follow the same course that John Belushi's did. Instead, Robin began all over again, with a new life, a new stable marriage, and a new growing career in movies.

These days Robin isn't afraid to be serious. He has a gentle, humble manner when he addresses the concerns that mean the most to him. But some critics wonder if this new happier Robin has lost his "edge." Maybe, they wonder, Robin's desperate need to prove himself was what drove him to be so frantically funny; maybe what made him so irresistible in the past was that he always seemed to be on the edge of losing control of the manic child inside of him.

That scared and desperately funny child once ruled Robin's life. In an interview with *Esquire* in 1989, Robin admitted to the existence of this frightened child inside him. "The fear of abandonment—the oldest, deepest fear of all: I'm ditched, I'm history. But . . . you begin to know you'll survive. . . . I can't deny the child, because obviously it's done kind of nice for me."

Clearly, the child in Robin Williams is alive and well. If he weren't, then Robin's house wouldn't be the sort of place it is—and Robin wouldn't be the enormously funny and creative person he still is.

And Robin isn't worried that he will lose his talent. When he gets up in front of people, he told *Us,* "I still get that feeling of: There are no boundaries. I just did a benefit the other night in Vegas, and it was wild because I hadn't been on in front of a large group of people in a long time. And people said I came on like . . . a rodeo pony." Apparently, Robin doesn't need any more new beginnings. "My career," he told the *Allentown Morning Call,* "is in a place where I can do anything except be hairless." He's at a point in his life where he can build on the gifts from his past.

One of these gifts is his feeling of comfort in the city of San Francisco. "Ever since I came here when I was 16, it

Robin Williams pauses in a park, as photographers clamor for a photo. He has put his early troubles behind him, and established himself as one of the most popular entertainers today.

just felt so free," Robin told *Us* in 1999, when he was asked about his adopted home city. "It's a combination of the mountains nearby, the ocean—all that. And the people. It's a very strange and kind of eclectic place. I don't stand out here—there's enough strange people. . . . It's a great city for me to walk around. I can go anywhere."

Robin seems to have also found the same freedom professionally that he finds in his home city. He not only continues to take on a wider and wider range of roles but also turns up in cameo roles in many movies. He's filmed bits in *The Adventures of Baron Munchausen; To Wong Foo, Thanks for Everything, Julie Newmar; Nine Months;* and

The Secret Agent. Robin told the *Allentown Morning Call* that he enjoys these cameo appearances. "It's quite extraordinary because I'm not under pressure to sell these movies. It's freeing. As time goes on and I get older and furrier, all that will be left for me will be the character parts. Character parts and the starring role in *Koko: The Musical.*"

Robin Williams can laugh at anything—and now his ability to laugh at himself as well indicates the true freedom that he has finally found. He no longer has to desperately prove himself. He knows who he is—a skilled artist, a father, a husband. Like the characters he so often plays, he's a little different from anyone else. But that's part of the fun. He likes being that person.

CHRONOLOGY

1952   Born to Robert and Laurie Williams on July 21

1969   Father Robert Williams retires and moves his family to Tiburon in northern California

1970   Enrolls in Claremont Men's College in southern California and takes his first theater course

1971   Enrolls in Marin Junior College near San Francisco

1973   Enrolls in Julliard School in New York in September; suffers a mental breakdown while at Julliard in December

1976   Leaves Julliard and returns to California, where he gets his start in stand-up comedy

1977   Cast in the revival of TV's *Laugh-In,* which flops; appears on *The Richard Pryor Show,* another flop

1978   Appears as Mork in an episode of Happy Days in February; marries Valerie Velardi in June; *Mork and Mindy* makes its debut on network television in September

1980   Appears in *Popeye,* his first starring role in a feature film

1982   Shares cocaine with comedian John Belushi hours before Belushi's death from a drug overdose March 2; *The World According to Garp* is released

1984   Becomes the father of Zachary; stars in *Moscow on the Hudson,* his first commercially successful movie

1986   Separates from Valerie Velardi; stars in the first telecast of "Comic Relief," a benefit to aid homeless people, on March 29

1987   Wins Emmy Award for his role on a Carol Burnett TV special; stars in *Good Morning, Vietnam* and earns his first Academy Award nomination

1988   Father Robert Williams dies in February; sued by an ex-girlfriend who claims he infected her with herpes. The case is eventually settled out of court

1989   Stars in *Dead Poets Society* and earns his second Academy Award nomination; marries Marsha Garges on April 30

1991   Earns his third Academy Award nomination for *The Fisher King*; stars in *Hook,* directed by Stephen Spielberg

1992   Appears on *The Tonight Show* May 22, as one of Johnny Carson's last guests

1993   Stars in *Mrs. Doubtfire,* the first movie produced by Blue Wolf Productions, the company he formed with wife Marsha

1994   Plays the roles of five different people through 10,000 years of history in the film *Being Human*

1995   Stars in *Jumanji*, which becomes a big hit and is spun off into an animated television series; makes cameo appearances in the films *To Wong Foo, Thanks for Everything, Julie Newmar* and *Nine Months*

1996   Stars with Nathan Lane in the hit *The Birdcage;* plays a 10-year-old boy who is aging prematurely in *Jack;* lends his voice to the genie in Disney's *Aladdin and the King of Thieves;* makes a cameo appearance in *The Secret Agent,* which is based on a novel by Joseph Conrad; appears in *Hamlet*

1997   Teams up with friend Billy Crystal in *Fathers' Day;* appears in *Flubber* and in Woody Allen's film *Deconstructing Harry*

1998   Stars in *Good Will Hunting, Patch Adams,* and *What Dreams May Come;* wins Academy Award for Best Supporting Actor for *Good Will Hunting* in March

1999   Makes *Jakob the Liar* and *Bicentennial Man*

FILMOGRAPHY

Can I Do It . . . Til I Need Glasses?, 1977

Popeye, 1980

The World According to Garp, 1982

The Survivors, 1983

Moscow on the Hudson, 1984

The Best of Times, 1986

Club Paradise, 1986

Seize the Day, 1986

Dear America: Letters Home from Vietnam, 1987 (voiceover)

Good Morning, Vietnam, 1987

The Adventures of Baron Munchausen, 1989 (cameo)

Dead Poets Society, 1989

Cadillac Man, 1990

Awakenings, 1990

Dead Again, 1991

The Fisher King, 1991

Hook, 1991

FernGully . . . The Last Rainforest, 1992

Aladdin, 1992

Mrs. Doubtfire, 1993

Being Human, 1994

To Wong Foo, Thanks For Everything, Julie Newmar, 1995 (cameo)

Nine Months, 1995 (cameo)

Jumanji, 1995

The Birdcage, 1996

Jack, 1996

Aladdin and the King of Thieves, 1996

The Secret Agent, 1996 (cameo)

Hamlet, 1996

Fathers' Day, 1997

Flubber, 1997

Deconstructing Harry, 1997

Good Will Hunting, 1998

Patch Adams, 1998

What Dreams May Come, 1998
Jakob the Liar, 1999
Bicentennial Man, 1999

FURTHER READING

Dougan, Andy. *Robin Williams.* New York: Thunder's Mouth Press, 1998.

Marshall, Garry. *Wake Me When It's Funny.* Holbrook, Mass.: Adams Publishing, 1995.

O'Neil, Thomas. *The Emmys.* New York: Penguin Books, 1992.

Reeve, Christopher. *Still Me.* New York: Random House, 1998.

Spignesi, Stephen J. *The Robin Williams Scrapbook.* Secaucus, N.J.: Citadel Press, 1997.

Weiner, Ed. *The TV Guide Book.* New York: HarperPerennial, 1992.

Winters, Jonathan. *Jonathan Winters into the '90s.* Studio City, Calif.: Dove Books, 1990.

Woodward, Bob. *Wired: The Short Life and Fast Times of John Belushi.* New York: Simon and Schuster, 1984.

APPENDIX

ORGANIZATIONS THAT DEAL WITH COCAINE ADDICTION OR SUBSTANCE ABUSE

COCAINE ADDICTION

Cocaine Anonymous World Service Office
P.O. Box 2000
Los Angeles, CA 90049-8000
Phone: (310) 559-5833
Fax: (310) 559-2554

24-hour Cocaine Hotline
*provides treatment referrals and
    information*
1-800-COCAINE

SUBSTANCE ABUSE HOTLINES

Al-Anon/Alateen Family Group
1-800-344-2666

Alcohol Treatment Referral Hotline
1-800-ALCOHOL

**Alcoholics Anonymous World Services
    Inc.**
(212) 870-3400

Center for Substance Abuse Treatment
referral service
1-800-662-HELP

Marijuana Anonymous World Services
1-800-766-6779

Nar-Anon Family Groups
(310) 547-5800

Narcotics Anonymous
(818) 773-9999

**National Council on Alcoholism and Drug
    Dependence Hopeline**
1-800-622-2255

Rational Recovery Systems
1-800-303-CURE

Secular Organizations for Sobriety (SOS)
(310) 821-8430

SMART Recovery Self-Help Network
(216) 292-0220

INDEX

PICTURE CREDITS

HAL MARCOVITZ is an award-winning journalist for the *Allentown Morning Call* newspaper in Pennsylvania. Among his honors are the 1993 and 1996 Keystone Press Awards for column writing, which were awarded by the Pennsylvania Newspaper Publishers Association. His first book was the satirical novel *Painting the White House*. He makes his home in Chalfont, Pennsylvania, with his wife Gail and daughters Ashley and Michelle.

JAMES SCOTT BRADY serves on the board of trustees with the Center to Prevent Handgun Violence and is the vice chairman of the Brain Injury Foundation. Mr. Brady served as assistant to the president and White House press secretary under President Ronald Reagan. He was severely injured in an assassination attempt on the president, but remained the White House press secretary until the end of the administration. Since leaving the White House, Mr. Brady has lobbied for stronger gun laws. In November 1993, President Bill Clinton signed the Brady Bill, a national law requiring a waiting period on handgun purchases and a background check on buyers.